'A loving – and overdue– celebration of three giants of English management, whose shared background and values brought days of wonder to three provincial clubs'

Jonathan Northcroft *The Sunday Times*

BEN DOBSON

TOO GOOD
TO BE
FORGOTTEN

Three Wise Men
From Football's Golden Era

First published by Pitch Publishing, 2024

Pitch Publishing
9 Donnington Park,
85 Birdham Road,
Chichester,
West Sussex,
PO20 7AJ
www.pitchpublishing.co.uk
info@pitchpublishing.co.uk

A CIP catalogue record is available for this book
from the British Library.

ISBN 978 1 80150 685 4

Typesetting and origination by Pitch Publishing
Printed and bound in India by Replika Press Pvt. Ltd.

Contents

Legacy

With special thanks to Big Lawrie

for making those days at The Dell

so special and saddling me with

Saints for life

Acknowledgements

This book wouldn't have seen the light of day without significant support and detailed research. My name may be on the cover, but I'm hugely indebted to those who gave their time to talk to me and offer their recollections and insights.

In particular I would like to offer my thanks to the interviewees who contributed so willingly. To my friend Tony Woodcock and to John McGovern; to the Ipswich Town legends that are Allan Hunter, John Wark, Russell Osman and Bryan Hamilton – all your loquacious and humorous contributions made for a memorable afternoon; to the heroes of my Southampton-supporting youth in Mick Channon, Peter Rodrigues, Hughie Fisher, Paul Bennett and Steve Williams.

A big thank you to the fans who contributed – Tim Smith the Tractor Boy, David Dykes, 60-plus years a Saint, and Richard Collier for his memories of Nottingham Forest's triumphant homecomings. And to fellow author and marvellous storyteller Michael Channon Jnr, thanks for the memories you shared and the fact that yours were interrupted by marginally fewer expletives than those of your father. The book is as much about the fans who experienced this special time as it is about those who instigated it.

A special thank you to Jonathan Northcroft of the *Sunday Times*, who has forgotten more about sports writing than I'll ever know and whose unfailing encouragement and sage advice have been invaluable.

Thank you to all at Pitch, my publishers, for the belief, professionalism and expertise.

Finally, thank you to my patient wife Mary for happily, perhaps *too* happily, losing me and Lex the dog to the study for hours on end and for suffering the endless pieces of paper and literature littering the house.

Every one of you has made this project enjoyable and fulfilling as well as possible. Thank you.

Foreword

Robson ... Clough ... McMenemy ...

I was sitting in a restaurant when I was first invited to write a foreword to *Too Good to Be Forgotten*, in Brighton – Victoria, Australia, not Brighton, Sussex, UK – and I was in the middle of a meal in a Japanese restaurant called Oushou. I was with my wife and some friends, one of which was a successful sports psychologist who was spending a lot of time working in India for one of the IPL cricket teams. I mentioned the book, the background and the characters to Dave, all of whom he had heard about and could relate to very easily, and I mentioned I had been asked to write a foreword and that I was thinking of mentioning the 'working-class' era of the 70s and 80s. Dave halted me mid-sentence and said, 'First you'll have to explain what working class is!' He felt that a big audience of readers would be too young to understand what the working class was or represented.

So ...

'Working class' is a socioeconomic term used to describe persons in a social class marked by jobs that provide low pay, require limited skill or physical labour. Typically, working-class jobs have reduced educational requirements. Some would say if the cap fits, wear it, and Mr Robson, Mr Clough and Mr McMenemy were extremely proud of where they came from and where they grew up.

I know from working under Sir Bobby Robson just how much his own upbringing influenced how he dealt with the players that he managed in later life. But Sir Bobby was a different manager when he finished at Newcastle United in 2004 than he was when I first joined Ipswich nearly 30 years earlier in 1975. The hard part of management is being able to change with the times; Mr Robson, Mr Clough and Mr McMenemy went from 70s football with punches being thrown regularly and only one substitute sat on the bench to the full-blown Premier League and international superstar scene.

I regularly watched Mr Clough's Derby County team of the late 60s and early 70s with the likes of Kevin Hector, Alan Hinton, Colin Todd, Roy McFarland, and by 1975 I was an apprentice at Mr Robson's Ipswich Town, with Hunter, Beattie, Mills and Whymark, to name a few. It wasn't long before I was playing against Southampton and Mr McMenemy's side, which included Alan Ball, Chris Nicholl, Channon and Keegan as a few of their stars.

Great players, playing great football, for great football clubs, managed by truly great man-managers.

This is the story of all of those things. Enjoy it – it is a tale worth telling.

Russell Osman

Suffolk, September 2023

A Word From Lawrie

I still feel great affection when I reflect on the times Cloughie, Bobby and myself spent together. We had so much in common and got on so well – good friends from a similar background. We would share some fun when our teams met, but also when we went to other matches and saw little of the game as we chatted away. Then there were the evenings away from football, taking in Sinatra or some other show. I very much doubt this goes on today.

This book is awash with happy memories of a closeness with players and public alike. I'll always be pleased that what we achieved touched local people who still want to talk about those times with me today. After the cup final, even those who didn't go to matches wanted to stop and say hello, proud that the name of Southampton was suddenly everywhere. In my native North East football was, and is, a passion which meant a few poor results would result in some less than complimentary greetings; in Southampton it was somehow closer, with people always happy for the opportunity to shake your hand. The bond formed then lasts for me to this day and I've made my happy home in the area for over half a century.

The three of us achieved much in the game which I think has legacy – not least the youth policies we established that continue to deliver today and our involvement in the creation of the League Managers' Association, but this relationship with the places and their people matters just as much.

I'm pleased *Too Good to Be Forgotten* pays due credit to the support we had from our boards and families. At Southampton I called my employers my 'olde worlde' directors. These were local people who represented the area and whose businesses contributed to its prosperity. They were directors, not 'owners' which is the word I always hear today and somehow that connection feels lost.

These were special days – too good to be forgotten indeed. Never say never, but I sense the game we have now is unlikely to allow anything quite the same to ever happen again. Times change and there is no disgrace in that, but nor is there in remembering what went before.

I think Bobby and Brian would agree that much of our character and method was formed in the North East and by those who instilled in us certain values we took into our management, but the places we went and the first-time successes we were able to share there are things I for one will cherish forever.

I hope you enjoy the memories here as I do.

Lawrie McMenemy,
Romsey, Hampshire 2023

Frontispiece

This is a story about place and time viewed through the prism of three football men who shared so much and realised unprecedented glories. It's also one of community and of leadership. It's a football book, but also concerned with more than football or, at least, more than just results. The achievements and legacies of these men demand a different measure and should never be erased.

It's both romantic in its unapologetic nostalgia for an era that can surely never come again, and practical in its recognition of the lessons in man-management and leadership, which remain relevant today in the field of sport and beyond.

It's about the place from which the three men *hailed* and how this formed them and became the bedrock of their future success. It's about the places they *went*, which became their adopted homes and were put on the map as never before and remain forever grateful.

It's about the time in which they grew up and that developed their characters, and about the period in which they challenged football's accepted order with three provincial clubs – a time that remains precious to many as a golden age of football to which we can't now return. It's a paean for a special period in the history of our wonderful game, allied to a certain melancholy and a distrust of what lies ahead.

It's about three men who shared values that would underpin their management and leadership and produce extraordinary results, for ten years delivering the remarkable as everyday.

Foremost among these was a common understanding of the importance of community and a deeply held conviction that what they achieved should be about more than just trophies. They would never forget their own roots. They were men of the people who never lost their connection to the background they shared within a football-obsessed region of the country, or to its people, to which they remain forever wedded. They would never undervalue the strength and dignity of the working man. That their footballing achievements with three 'small' clubs not only delivered magical moments of euphoria for their supporters and players, bringing pleasure to countless thousands, but left a lasting sense of pride, status and gratitude within in their wider communities – truly the time of their lives – gave them an immense, if largely unspoken, satisfaction.

This, notwithstanding or disregarding the cups and the glory, is the real story of these three men and why they, their achievements and those times of our lives they made possible are too good to be forgotten.

Prologue

Sliding Doors

'What's meant to be will always find a way.'

Trisha Yearwood, musician

Moments matter. In any story of success, particularly sustained success, an element of fate or good fortune is highly probable. Three matches, three apparently unremarkable ones in unremarkable settings, would contribute to the writing of a history that couldn't have been the same without them. Then again, as the American author Marissa Meyer suggested, 'Maybe there isn't such a thing as fate – maybe it's just the opportunities we're given, and what we do with them.'

Saturday, 3 January 1976, The Dell, Southampton, 4.45pm
It's the sort of unfulfilling, cold, dark, post-New Year celebration late afternoon beloved of a British January and it feels like one ripe for going through the motions. In which case, Southampton's footballers are playing their part to the letter. The FA Cup third round is still a weekend that can temporarily lift the post-festive gloom at a time when the competition reigns supreme across the world in domestic club football. It's the moment when everyone gets the chance to dream again that, this year, a footballing fairy tale might yet be made real.

At the same stage 12 months previously, Saints had been awoken rudely from their own dream almost before they'd had chance to turn out the light, through a home defeat to West Ham. Up to now they haven't wintered well this year either. Today they're drifting, with a sense of gentle inevitability, towards the same fate at the hands of Aston Villa. Rather than serious discontent, The Dell crowd gives off an air of unsurprised resignation. I know this because I'm sitting in among them in the seat that came with my first-ever season ticket – the one I had unwrapped just nine days previously.

Lawrie McMenemy must be feeling both the cold and the ennui all around him as he hunches his guardsman's frame into the bunker-like home dugout. This is not how things were supposed to be. In 18 months as Southampton manager since succeeding the club legend that was Ted Bates – in the eyes of many supporters as a most surprising, underwhelming and underserving choice – he had done little to disprove the doubters. Relegation to the Second Division in his first season hit him so hard that even his increasingly recognisable personality was struggling to fend off the stigma attached to that achievement. It left him feeling a total failure. The planned and expected immediate return to the top tier the following season had ended in 13th place and, worse, this offcomer had had the impertinence to transfer the fans' favourite – club captain and 1966 World Cup England player Terry Paine – out of the club in an act that to supporters at the time appeared clear evidence that he was not the man for the job.

He had spent the season running the gauntlet of a chorus of boos at the normally genteel Dell, the cramped confines of which must have made the disapproval seem more vitriolic than it really was. Now, midway through his third season, although a run of five successive wins has lifted the team to fourth in the league, the eight matches they've already lost in the first 18 of the campaign are a better barometer of the consistent inconsistency for which McMenemy's team is becoming renowned – one sprinkled with the stardust of several internationals who struggle to find either the right approach or motivation for the perceived mundanities of the Second Division – and which suggests, correctly, that promotion won't be forthcoming this season either.

McMenemy is aware of, and supremely grateful for, the steadfast backing of his board but as Saints are heading out of the treasured competition with a whimper for the second year running, his vision of the future at Southampton – both his and that he envisaged for the club – seems somehow to have got lost. Another early exit, allied to failure in the promotion ambition, might yet have potentially serious repercussions, loyal board of directors or not. The apathetic atmosphere around him now may be weighing even more heavily on his broad shoulders than the animosity had done previously. Resignation rather than consternation has become the dominant emotion for the club's fans. He needs something – anything – to happen, and it's hard to conceive of Saints' and McMenemy's journey ahead should the next few minutes never have happened.

The match has run on aimlessly into injury time with Villa still 1-0 ahead and barely threatened. Few hearts start to beat faster as the ball rolls across the path of Hughie Fisher – fantastic club servant, top-class human being, but very much one of McMenemy's 'road sweepers' rather than the match-saver required in this moment. His strike isn't the sweetest ever witnessed and the chances of it making it through the forest of legs inhabiting the penalty area resemble those of a high handicapper trying to reach the green from deep within the trees. But bobble through it does, landing low in the corner of John Burridge's net and giving the author his first-ever experience of the rush that comes with a late, late goal. It's as remarkable as it is unexpected. When the rush subsides, however, it also feels like no more than a stay of execution prior to the replay to come on the First Division club's home pitch.

Three months and 28 days later Southampton will be holding aloft the FA Cup and, along with it, experiencing what the journalist Jeremy Wilson would refer to as the beginning of the cult of McMenemy. In an instant he has become a made man. An untouchable. Things are never going to be quite the same again. Moments matter.

Saturday, 18 February 1978, Eastville Stadium, Bristol, 4.40pm
Another FA Cup Saturday, the likes of which seem forever lost in the 1970s. Ipswich's fifth-round tie at Bristol Rovers wouldn't have made it as far as the coin toss in the modern game, the pitch covered in snow and players trying to keep their feet like seven-year-olds in wellingtons attempting to negotiate stepping stones in a river for the first time. Here was a classic FA Cup giant-killing tableau.

Bobby Robson is beginning to turn the tide at Ipswich. Top-six finishes in the First Division in each of the previous five seasons suggest nothing less. A talented young squad, the majority of which has grown up together and been schooled through Robson's scouting system, youth teams and reserve team, is playing football that's winning praise throughout the game. There's a sense, however, that Robson needs something concrete soon. His obsession with the game stokes a burning desire to be a winner and he wants tangible evidence of this to stand alongside the increasing nationwide affection for him and his club. The naked truth is that Robson has now been at Ipswich for nearly nine years. A single Texaco Cup, important as that will be in the longer-term story of the club, is not a return with which Robson can be satisfied. His fervent passion needs the outlet of a major trophy if he's to provide the people of the town with the ultimate success for which he yearns.

And by this February things are regressing rather than progressing, with little sign that he's marshalling a group of talented young men with their greatest triumphs yet before them. Ahead of this cup tie at Eastville, Ipswich sit 17th in the First Division. They're still occasionally punching above their weight and enjoying more of the memorable nights that are to become part of the club's folklore, with Europe again to the fore, having seen them beat the Barcelona of Johan Cruyff 3-0 at Portman Road the previous autumn. But elimination from both the League Cup and UEFA Cup within a week in December, allied to a by now most unaccustomed struggle around the relegation zone, means there's only one route left to a successful season and to maintaining the club's run of European adventures. Robson wants – perhaps needs – that elusive major trophy, and soon.

Conditions, the home crowd and the match's momentum are all conspiring against Robson and his team. Their first-half lead has been turned over through two scrappy goals from corners, which prove almost impossible to defend on the ice rink that the crowded Ipswich penalty area has become. Now 2-1 behind well into the second half, Rovers knock the ball long into the Ipswich left-back channel and suddenly striker Bobby Gould is in on goal. 'A chance for Bobby Gould to wrap it up ... and he's taken it!' shouts the HTV West commentator with something rather less than impartiality. The fact that the ball has been played to Gould off the Ipswich defender has escaped the linesman, who erroneously raises his flag to disallow the goal that would have ended Robson's cup run in that moment.

Minutes from time, Robin Turner, who has never scored for Ipswich, somehow stays on his feet long enough to skew a cross against a post from three yards out when hitting the net might have been considered more straightforward. The ball finds a generous angle off the upright that permits it to trickle over the line. Ipswich win the replay comfortably and fewer than three months later Robson is sleeping with the FA Cup under his bed, and his adopted town is embarking on the greatest party in its history.

Saturday, 14 May 1977, Burnden Park, Bolton, 4.45pm British
Summer Time/Palma airport, Mallorca 5.45pm CET

'Life is what happens to us while we're busy making other plans,' John Lennon would sing in 'Beautiful Boy' three years later. These weren't actually his own words but those of the American writer Allen Saunders 20 years before but, either way, it's not believed they were penned to immortalise the manner of Nottingham Forest's unlikely promotion to the First Division. However, had they been, nobody could have argued that they weren't apposite.

Three minutes into injury time and the ball is launched into the Wolves penalty area for the fourth time in a frantic minute. The three Bolton players in the six-yard box are all millimetres from applying the touch that will draw the match, but goalkeeper Gary Pierce's desperate grab for the ball succeeds and the full-time whistle puts an end to Bolton's ten-minute Charge of the Light Brigade. The 1976/77 Second Division season is effectively over …

… and with that whistle comes perhaps the clearest proof that outrageous fortune often plays as important a role as strategy and managerial acumen in achieving success. It concerns the role of fate, or at least good fortune, in the emergence of Nottingham Forest. Given Brian Clough's undoubted gifts as a manager, this is not to say a period of success wouldn't have been forthcoming anyway, but the reality is that a league title in 1978 and two European Cups in the two subsequent years wouldn't have happened at all without the intervention of a third party outside Clough's control.

After 18 months in the Second Division since his arrival, similar in their lack of any apparent dramatic progress to those of McMenemy, in 1976/77 Forest are finally starting to respond to their manager's methods and are at last a serious player in the promotion race. That said, they've never been in pole position. For much of the season they've trailed Ian Greaves's talented Bolton team (which had just missed out on promotion the previous year and is generally regarded as one of the strongest in the division and the one most worthy of going up) in pursuit of third place. Then the spectre of Bolton's collapse of the previous year, when they managed just five wins and 14 points from their last 15 matches to miss out on promotion by a point, begins to haunt them. Now they go on a run of only four wins and 14 points from 14 matches up to 7 May, the day on which Forest have completed their season by winning at home to Millwall.

But an FA Cup campaign full of replays means Bolton still have several matches in hand and, despite their recent run, they require just three points from their last two matches – at home to already promoted Wolves, and a trip to the safe-from-relegation but far from dangerous Bristol Rovers. Neither opponent, therefore, with much to play for. It's still Bolton's for the taking and take it they're widely expected to do. Even a point against Wolves and they'll be firm favourites. It's assumed the Wolves players will be 'on the beach', which in the true manner of Clough, with his season finished and no more that can be done, is exactly where he and his squad are heading, on a flight to Mallorca as the result comes through. Bolton 0 Wolves 1. Forest promoted.

Years later, Tony Woodcock is unequivocal: 'That changed everything – that moment as we got off the plane. It allowed us to start strengthening in a way I'm pretty sure we wouldn't have done otherwise – Shilton, Gemmill, Burns. The rest is history.' Indeed. Three years later Forest were English and double European champions. The sliding doors had opened for Clough, and he was about to charge right on through them …

Two Weeks in Spring

Saturday, 22 April 1978
Nottingham Forest are at Coventry City in the spring sunshine. The *Match of the Day* cameras are here to watch Peter Shilton

defy the opposition as he has been doing all season. Every week since their arrival back in the First Division the sages have been predicting the Forest bubble will burst. Liverpool's European champions have the pedigree and the experience to reel in and overtake Clough's upstarts when the pressure comes on. But today will be the day that puts an end to all such predictions. To many it still appears something of a mystery as to how we've arrived at this moment. Promoted teams don't win the title. And yet, with a 0-0 draw, Clough and his team secure that very prize. For the second time in seven seasons, he has worked the oracle. He isn't finished yet.

Saturday, 29 April 1978

Southampton have been languishing in the Second Division for four years, their team of cup-winning rascals unsuited to the slog of a lower league promotion campaign. It's not where Lawrie McMenemy wanted to or expected to be five years into the job. On the previous Tuesday night his team secured a point at Orient and celebrated as if the promotion goal had been achieved. With a significantly superior goal difference to their nearest challengers Brighton, even defeat on the last day and a Brighton win would require a massive goal swing to deny them.

As a young fan I'm not nearly so sanguine. Visions of a heavy home defeat and a remarkable turnaround lurk within. But, as it happens, Saints' opponents on another beautiful spring afternoon are Tottenham ... and both teams need just a point to be sure of promotion at Brighton's expense. To this day, the 0-0 draw played out at a rather serene pace with post-match handshakes all round is still considered by the Brighton supporters to be the Second Division's greatest-ever stitch-up. Neither I nor, I suspect, Lawrie McMenemy cared. He had righted the calamity of that relegation in his first season; now, with an FA Cup already in his cabinet, he was back. The cult of McMenemy continued to grow.

Saturday, 6 May 1978

More sunshine. In fact, this time, more sizzling summer heat than bright spring afternoon. All the pre-match preamble and anticipation of a 1970s FA Cup Final – still the most coveted club trophy in world football (at a pinch, the European Cup its only rival) – the classic end-of-season showpiece of that era with 100,000 in the stadium and many millions more watching across the globe. For the first time in their history Ipswich Town adorn such a stage. The increasing promise and plaudits of the previous few seasons have led them here – a culmination of the unstinting effort Bobby Robson has invested to turn the club around. But in nine years he has no major trophy to offer real validation. Few expect it to arrive today. Football's accepted way of the world still considers Ipswich as the plucky unfashionables from the shires, up against the metropolitan might of Arsenal. But following Southampton's lead two years before, Ipswich ignore the theory and the predictions. Roger Osborne's second-half goal wins them the cup. They're a degree more fashionable tonight.

* * *

Two weeks; three Saturdays; three moments of remarkable achievement. Three provincial clubs upsetting the natural order of things. Three inspirational leaders of men have made it happen. Ultimately, their levels of success measured in trophies wouldn't be identical. Their methods shared many traits but occasionally diverged to reflect the individuality of each man and his personality. But each in their own way would leave a special and lasting legacy. They were going on to achieve similarly and differently incredible things.

Introduction

Too Good To Be Forgotten

'It's about the memories you create. That's what an enriched life is.'

Justin Rose, European Ryder Cup golfer

Is it wrong to love the past as much as the future? If so, I offer up to derision my abiding nostalgia. I don't believe I'm mired forever in what has gone before, but I understand its value and the role great moments and shifting sands from another time play in creating, layer upon layer, the fabric of sport. I accept change as an immutable truth and that the matches we follow are bound to evolve and adapt in concert with the society in which they exist. But it's a universally valid fact that much of the richness in the sports we follow lie in their traditions and their immortals. Perhaps the wish to recall them emanates from a hope that it will make us all feel immortal by association.

The contradiction between appreciating what the modern game offers us and the sense nevertheless that something special from its past has been lost forms a core part of this book, which recognises that while the wisest counsel probably lies somewhere in between, what came before is the canvas on which today's picture was laid down.

Too Good to Be Forgotten lands primarily in the years 1975–1985, which were my formative years following football. Personally indulgent, yes, but such nostalgia is intrinsic in our affection for sport. Regular watching becomes an addiction and delivers unshakeable memories that, in this case for me, are no less vivid for being nearly half a century old. So, while this specific time period may mean different things to different people, I see it through the rose-tinted spectacles that were the eyes of my youth.

These ten years also bestowed upon us three football men whose remarkable deeds positively affected the well-being of individuals and communities and were responsible for the last – surely the last-ever – sustained breaking of the football mould. This is therefore fundamentally a celebration of three of football's own immortals and an assessment of why what they achieved during these treasured footballing years mattered as it did. It also intends to convey a premonitory sense of loss that such a thing is unlikely ever to happen in this way again. The outstanding sportswriter and Brian Clough biographer, Duncan Hamilton, wrote in his elegy for red ball cricket, *One Long Beautiful Summer*, that his objective, like that of the photographer, was to capture a moment and hold it immobile. To capture this particular time forever, that we may return to and savour its memories, is my purpose here too. The bewildering pace of life today, and that of the changes to our game, mean we often don't appreciate what we have until it has passed us by and, in this case in particular, I find myself of the same mind as Mr Hamilton – that we didn't perhaps realise how historic this time was while we were living it. So, I'm going back there now to offer it my gratitude.

I was ensnared as a Southampton fan at an early age, and my love of football was formed at The Dell in a timespan that almost precisely bookended the Lawrie McMenemy years. I'm approaching 50 years and 87 per cent of my days on Earth, as one of those supporters who is unfathomably incapable of shedding my allegiance despite the disappearance of all my connections to the place itself – no home there, no family, few friends with whom contact remains from the years gone by, and no trips to St Mary's itself. In fact, I've never actually set foot inside that stadium, the move to which was deemed essential 22 years ago to the goal of survival in the wild seas of the Premier League as the superyachts of Manchester City and their elite companions swept off over the horizon, but that fundamentally changed my club and my relationship with it. What's more, and inevitably in the end, it didn't work for a club clinging like a man on a cliff face to an unrealistic ambition of competitiveness in such an environment. Perhaps my staying away today is part of a desire, conscious or otherwise, to preserve the memories of The Dell and the glorious and now untouchable moments it gave me. For today the possibility of repeating the sustained success of those ten years has been taken away from unfashionable, provincial clubs for what may prove to be an eternity.

I know times move on but, for me, in dismantling the wooden West Stand in which I used to sit and stamp my feet in time with the raucous renditions of 'Oh When the Saints …', and the bricks of the Milton Road End on which I first experienced the cordite thrill and latent menace of a packed terrace, they also began to dismantle something of the club's soul and slowly but surely its relationship with its community. In putting together this book I spoke with fans of Ipswich Town and Nottingham Forest as clubs that also had their significant time in the sun in those years, and their mourning of that loss was the same as my own.

I said I retain no connection, but actually one remains – that born of happy memories. This is the umbilical cord that keeps us attached and the answer to that puzzle of enduring, unconditional allegiance. The memories don't all have their source in the highest-profile moments and the greatest successes in the record books; they're a myriad of the apparently insignificant – in my case perhaps a Peter Osgood header, an Ivan Golac volley or even a particular record from that week's Top 40 coming over the tannoy as I emerged into the light at the top of the stairs in the West Stand Upper to be greeted by the greenest of pitches on a sunny matchday. These little things pile upon each other like snowflakes in a drift to form a recollection of the time when football offered *all* fans the chance to dream and a bond between place, players and club that meant more than silverware. They also engender a grieving for a game forever changed by its modern incarnation's obsession with the price of everything and the value of nothing.

When Saints were relegated from the top division in 2005 I was devastated, even as a supposedly well-adjusted 38-year-old. So, should it not concern me that when defeat at home to Fulham while writing this book consigned them to the same fate 18 years on, I had no such feeling of desolation? Why not? Because the Valhalla of the financially rich but morally bankrupt construct that is the Premier League is my Frankenstein's monster. The desperation in the struggle each season not to meet a fate we're told is so dire – dire enough that a sporting outcome is hauled away from its appropriate perspective – has become a chore and a drudge, making recollection of those halcyon days all the more poignant. At the same time I was delighted that Nottingham Forest survived, even if I have no envy of their desire and peak ambition of 17th place next season. I'm equally happy that Ipswich have come up a division and we'll be able to renew old rivalries and share stories of happy days at the true football ground that is Portman Road. I retain a fondness for these teams and a kinship with their fans born of shared experiences and mutual understanding. For these were clubs that achieved astonishing things under the guidance of three wise men and in doing so delivered a status and a pride that changed communities. As Justin's Rose's words above suggest, a life is enriched when special memories are created. This is what these three men brought to the lives of many, which is the fundamental reason for this long thank-you note.

What follows is therefore an attempt to relive a football era now lost in the mists of time and do due credit to that last breaking of the football mould and the special men who made it happen.

Three Wise Men

The phenomenon of three men from the same background coming to prominence at the same time by dint of their football management abilities isn't unique. Leo Moynihan and Jonny Owen's excellent book and documentary, *The Three Kings*, tell the story of Bill Shankly, Matt Busby and Jock Stein, three legendary managers born and brought up in close proximity around the city of Glasgow, and their resurrection of three sleeping-giant football clubs.

Shankly, Busby and Stein indisputably stand four-square as hugely significant managers in the game's history. Lawrie McMenemy acknowledged this, and the link to our 'Three Wise Men', in his autobiography: 'Jock Stein was a league above my managerial era. His included Shanks and Don Revie and Sir Matt Busby. Ours would be Brian Clough, Bobby Robson, and myself. All dominated eras with their approach to coaching and preparing their teams.'

The achievement of the three Scots was, however, in resurrecting clubs and cities that had such status, recognition and resource that they were always destined to take their places at the top of the game at some point and sustain it for a long period thereafter. For many reasons, while those three managers have rightly been lauded to the skies, the achievements of their three successors from the north-east of England may be fit to rank alongside or even exceed them. The journalist and writer Simon Barnes certainly thought so in the case of Clough in the period from 1977 to 1980, saying, 'If you factor in Forest's playing and financial resources, these three years can be regarded as the greatest achievement by any manager of an English club.' If there was something in the whisky north of the border, perhaps it infected brown ale as well.

It would be hard to argue that not enough has been written about Brian Clough (except, I imagine, by Cloughie himself) or that he has never received recognition for being, in the eyes of many, the greatest ever. Sir Bobby too, partly as a result of his time as England manager, the memories of Turin 1990, his notable successes abroad and his subsequent reincarnation as a national treasure during his time at his beloved Newcastle, has also been the subject of much outstanding football literature. Perhaps Lawrie hasn't had that same level of recognition and, with an acknowledgement that there may be an element of bias in this, given he was more responsible than most for the happiness of my childhood, I feel he deserves to have that addressed. McMenemy brought only one major trophy to Southampton ... does that justify his presence in such company? Well, yes, because the heart of this narrative is not just about what they *won* but, perhaps less definably, what they *did*. The trophies they did win were the passports to their longevity and footballing reputations, but to decry them for not winning more would miss the point.

Three clubs and communities in which even those who dwelt there believed they were preordained to drift along the backwaters with resignation but no great despondency, were transported into national and global consciousness and afforded a sense of pride that will endure forever for those who experienced it. For ten years McMenemy brought a profile and a pride to a previously sleepy football city and paraded a stream of star names before his club's fans, incongruous in the setting of The Dell, the like of which had never been seen before, has never been since and assuredly never will be again. For several years Saints fans watched with pride as the most exciting attacking team in the country was paraded before them. Given where this journey began, McMenemy is undoubtedly worthy of his place in the story. So, I want to revisit the evidence even if, in some cases, it has been done before. As John Arlott once suggested, weight of evidence never harmed any case and even to assemble the ingredients stirs warm memories.

Were these men indeed three of a kind or rather individuals simply meshed by their achievements? The parallels in their journeys are sufficient to suggest the former, not least by Clough himself who, in his autobiography, reflected on what bound them together: 'Funny how all three of us had things in common. All from the North East and all having success with relatively small, unfashionable clubs.' But given the frequency with which the words 'complete one-off' have been used in relation to Brian Clough by many respected people within the game, it would be a mistake to attempt to force-fit a contention that all three managers were identical (or that their achievements were all at the same level in terms of major trophy success). They were not. Similarities and differences appear throughout the analysis of each of the facets that made them great.

In the most simplistic terms, the synchronicities of timing and their statistical records are remarkable. McMenemy and Robson both began their league managerial careers in 1968. Clough started three years earlier at Hartlepool. Robson arrived at Ipswich (in 1969) several years before McMenemy at Southampton (1973) and Clough at Forest (January 1975), but his earlier departure means the overall details are strikingly similar. Their managerial records at these three clubs read as follows:

	Matches	Win%	Draw%	Loss%
Robson/Ipswich	657	42	25	33
McMenemy/ Southampton	604	42	27	31
Clough/Nottingham Forest	994	47	26	27

Over such an extended period the correlations are astounding. But what they achieved for three clubs of a very similar standing – unfashionable and unfancied on their arrival and somnolent when it came to football, lacking, at that point, the seething obsession with which the game teemed in many of the big cities and industrial heartlands – is borne out not purely by statistics. They took the pride they had in their own native community in the North East and bestowed something similar in those places where they were to become adopted sons and remain forever so. If there was one thing that truly bound them together, it was that they were valued in these places for more than just the football, and that this mattered to them. For a blissful period, they turned three sleepy provincial towns and cities into names recognisable at home and abroad. If this is the 'what', the 'how' navigates us through that mixture of shared traits and subtle differences. It suggests that while they were in some ways distinct in character and personality, they shared values that induced methods that would make them a fortune today.

There was a congruence in their backgrounds and the values and beliefs that their similar upbringings gave them. All were true sons of the North East, the children of hard-working men and women who instilled discipline and respect. There were no differences here. As a consequence, they were of similar character, but not indistinguishable.

The football journalist Bob Harris knew all three men well and in his opinion they were distinct. He saw Clough as unstable and unpredictable: 'Hard to judge because you couldn't get close to him.' Duncan Hamilton, who interviewed the man on many occasions, wrote of his personality: 'You could take nothing for granted. Like a hornet, he stung people indiscriminately.' He was the possessor of a divine impatience. Unlike McMenemy and Robson in Harris's experience: 'They were very approachable. With Lawrie, you got what was on the packaging – strong morally, he was a massive personality, and he built his career around that, whereas Bobby and Brian had built reputations through playing success.' One thing, however, did unite them in Harris's experience: 'They *all* had an ego.' Those egos gave them a certain aura, a power of personality, which was a key component in their being accepted at, and soon dominating, their clubs. All had media profiles and were adept at using these to gain publicity for their clubs – clubs used to being ignored – putting them in a spotlight whenever they could, which, for a while at least, their achievements scarcely deserved.

Clough's was clearly the most public profile, at a national television chat-show level that made him instantly recognisable whether you followed football or not. His personality was such that at times even now it's remembered almost to the exclusion of his teams' performances. McMenemy, through his personal impact both in physical stature and quick-witted humour, actually made his name on television before he did so through success on the pitch, although his presence was at a level below Clough's, mainly contained within football-specific programmes. While Robson did some TV work, he was less prominent, although still savvy as to how the media could help put his club on the map.

Their shared interests when occasionally away from football could bring the three together if time permitted them to be indulged, including Clough and Robson's love of cricket and the passion all three shared for Frank Sinatra (in Robson's case formed at an early age with his music being ever-present on the radiogram in his parents' living room), whom they all went to see at every available opportunity – sometimes together – and whose lyrics were regularly to be heard pouring forth from the manager's office at the City Ground. They proved over time that they had digested and learned from the words and the philosophy of 'My Way'.

None had the easiest of starts at the clubs they were to turn around, and success was far from instantaneous. They shared struggles in their earliest years, and if it were only Robson and McMenemy who felt under serious threat of the sack,

Clough's first 18 months at Forest might also be described as underwhelming – it wasn't all sunshine for him at Forest any more than it was for his contemporaries in their early days at Ipswich and Southampton. They each had to ride out some turbulent times, inevitably made some wrong decisions although more that were to be proved wise, and rarely any that didn't stem from conviction and enthusiasm.

As managers, Clough was easily the most vaunted and well known before their respective arrivals, and the fact that he had already dress-rehearsed his Forest magician's trick, by taking another unremarkable Second Division club in Derby County to promotion, the First Division title, and a European Cup semi-final before landing in Nottingham in 1975, is one reason his overall résumé of achievements sits above all others. His midfielder Martin O'Neill, one of those present at the club before Clough and who would go on to be a rather unlikely European champion, wasn't unaware of the figure coming through the door, referring to the instant personal impact afforded him by his major celebrity.

Clough's feats and reputation meant he commanded the more immediate respect, arriving as he did with his Derby successes under his belt. Robson and McMenemy possessed comparatively thin management CVs. Clough and Robson had enjoyed distinguished playing careers – both England internationals – and as such both had a degree of credibility on which to fall back when managing established players. This was not something available to McMenemy, whose brief, more journeyman career in the lower leagues was cut short by injury. As a result, he had to fight a longer battle to win player respect at the outset – a challenge that only the impact of that physical bearing and strength of personality, and ultimately the delivery of a first major trophy, would surmount. But Robson himself made the case for Lawrie indirectly when he pointed out that Arsène Wenger wasn't a great player, but Bobby Charlton was, so there was no hard-and-fast rule. In the era in which they began, they all had youth on their side relative to the majority of managers at the time. While initially that may have meant the fight for acceptance and respect required a little more effort and application of personality, it also gave a certain glamour and film-star sheen compared to those managing elsewhere who were longer in the tooth.

All three took on sleepy clubs, where the support took a different form from that in their own North East hotbeds, and shook them awake. This was only possible through several pillars of support – their employers, their families and their coaching staffs. Robson and McMenemy enjoyed what they termed 'gentlemen directors' who offered them both loyalty and autonomy. The relationships were strong, affectionate and encouraged a loyalty from the managers themselves, which would lead to both consistently turning down offers from admiring suitors. Clough's relationship with directors was of a different nature, and always had been, and stemmed from an inherent distrust of authority not evident in his two contemporaries. While he too acknowledged that the support of one particular Forest director was an important factor in what was to come, there was always a more suspicious and standoffish relationship between Clough and his boards, which was just the way he liked it. As John Arlott once wrote of the controversial television and radio presenter Gilbert Harding, 'He could be spectacularly rude but not necessarily for rudeness' sake, rather out of his own fundamental independence … which meant he was quite happy to be an outspoken minority of one on any subject.' Clough and Harding would have made for an interesting conversation.

There was total alignment in the strength of their family ties. The three were devoted family men who at their lowest ebbs found solace and support in their long-suffering wives – something that may not always have been afforded due credit for the longevity of their achievements. Every one of those relationships lasted a lifetime. All three also leaned on men they trusted as able lieutenants – in Clough's case, one effectively a partner who undoubtedly made him better.

They shared a vision of how the game should be played – that it should provide entertainment for those spending their hard-earned wages to come and watch, and that it was a simple game made over-complicated by too many people. If there *was* any divergence here, it was that Clough was even more dismissive of tactics and analysis of the opposition. His teams would always play their game regardless, whereas McMenemy and Robson would sometimes pick a team to do a specific job. McMenemy's deployment of man-marker Manny Andruszewski as an extra defender to nullify Tony Currie successfully in a cup semi-final was one example of a tactic Clough would have been unlikely to have considered necessary.

The most commonly referenced attributes within every interview undertaken for this book were a genius for man-management and an associated ability to create a togetherness that moved mountains. Over ten years they gave their teams and clubs their character, choosing their widely diverse members and creating for them an atmosphere of ease that was ultimately reflected in outstanding performance. They were all possessed of a sixth sense for how to get the very best out of the disparate personalities that populated their clubs and their dressing rooms. None was averse to trying the unorthodox and they shared in pioneering the idea of the mid-season break (even if the suspicion may linger that in the case of Clough and Peter Taylor this was as much to do with their own penchant for the sun and sea of Cala Millor as it was a genuine attempt to improve any title-winning chances).

But the way their genius for managing people expressed itself was explicit to each. Clough would look to do the unexpected at every turn, combining a strikingly open mind with a firm set of standards. For him it was about keeping his players guessing and on their toes. Complacency was the devil's work and another method of repelling it was to be more sparing and less obvious with praise, which meant, if and when it ever arrived, it had the effect of lifting people to the rafters. In his man-management he would treat all individuals the same way, whether they be Garry Birtles, the free transfer from Long Eaton, or the country's first-ever million-pound player, Trevor Francis. Clough changed for no one.

McMenemy, as perhaps befitted the dressing room he had assembled, was more pragmatic and willing to apply different strokes for different folks, indulging his 'rascals' if they performed on the pitch, while putting the fear of god into his apprentices and young first-teamers.

Robson, although several players attest to his toughness when required, was the most avuncular of the three and reached for the carrot more than the stick. While equally capable of a volcanic eruption, he made the arm-round-the-shoulder approach his primary modus operandi as a better fit for the needs of his young, primarily homegrown team. Both he and McMenemy were described as father figures by several of the players they developed. Although he may have taught them many life skills such as discipline and manners, not by any stretch of imaginative licence is this an epithet many would apply to Clough.

All three were supreme motivators, sharing an instinct for taking the right approach in any given circumstance – a knack of assessing the moment and employing the most effective motivational tool. It was built on three principles – giving and receiving trust, straight-talking and honesty, and a resultant building of confidence. That confidence was also boosted by their creation of a rock-solid togetherness. In return the players hitched their wagons to their manager's stars. And, in short, they were encouraged to have fun. This created a bond that remains to this day and can be seen in the number of players who have never left their respective communities – the feeling of connection also extending into those communities themselves. It was the pillar on which the teams would stand as greater than the sum of their parts.

However, despite their reputations as man-managers, Robson and McMenemy would bridle at any idea that they weren't also high-class coaches. Clough would protest less about this but could indeed coach in his own inevitably idiosyncratic way. Even if part of their 'simple game' philosophy was an ability to quickly identify a player's strengths, or potential strengths that others had missed, and then play to those strengths rather than trying to make players something they were not, each was also able to improve players almost without them knowing it. In *Bobby Robson: The Ultimate Patriot*, biographer Bob Harris summarises Robson as 'intelligent without being a super-intellectual, a great motivator of men without being the best coach in the world, he could inspire and more often than not he allowed his players to go out and express themselves'. If precisely the same words had been written about Clough or McMenemy, I doubt many would argue with them.

Tony Woodcock played for both Clough and Robson, the latter at international level, and although he didn't know McMenemy well, he met him enough to be able to offer me his own comparison:

> My experience of playing for them [Clough and Robson] was that they were clearly two successful managers, but they weren't the same. Cloughie was brash, loud, in your face when he walked through the door; Bobby generally wasn't that type of character. He was gentlemanly – very honest. Some players, to be honest, might have looked at his club record and thought, 'How did he do that?' but it was probably, like Cloughie, man-management and choosing the right players. Lawrie I didn't know that well, but he always came across as the Grenadier Guard and perhaps he

brought that element of the military to his football club. Choosing the players, and especially those who could handle their style of management and fitting the jigsaw together.

This ability to build teams, and to rebuild them, was another marked and shared skill but again characterised by differences of approach. Clough and Robson both built their most successful teams on solid defensive platforms, something that may explain their greater success in Europe, while McMenemy's penchant for the magic dust of star attacking players made for a more gung-ho style, ultimately of huge entertainment but less concrete success in terms of trophies. Each believed in, to use one of McMenemy's favourite phrases, the combination of 'violinists and road sweepers', and in using the latter, and the energy of youth, to be the legs for the stylists. McMenemy just used his string players rather more, that's all – at least until his 1984 incarnation when he became the first manager in the country to utilise a sweeper system regularly and found a defensive parsimony that if present in his earlier teams would surely have delivered a championship.

While McMenemy's most-renowned tool in team building was his ability to sell the club and entice players of exceptional ability and reputation – and to squeeze every last drop of their quality out of them – Clough did more by way of improving what he had already found at his disposal, supplemented when the time was right with clever, cost-effective signings of players with less stardust but with the abilities that he had identified he needed.

Of the three, it was Robson who leaned most heavily on youth and brought more players into his successful teams through his age-group and reserve teams, although all three would be prepared to trust young players in the most challenging of circumstances if they believed in their ability and felt that they could add value to the team. For it was all about the team; they may have gone about it in different ways but piecing together the jigsaw perceptively was common to each.

However, when it came to *rebuilding* teams there was a demonstrable difference. Robson and McMenemy created several different teams within this period, each slightly stronger and more effective than the last, seeking evolution rather than revolution. Clough readily admits to, and regrets, a casual dismantling of his great side of 1977–80 amid a flurry of bizarre, expensive and unsuccessful acquisitions, which departed radically from his previously tried-and-trusted and successful formula, with the result that, until he regathered himself post-Peter Taylor to create a much-admired young team in 1984, his success came solely through the one squad he relied upon, with the occasional tweak, in those three seasons.

In identifying the key moments in turning the tide, each would highlight the importance they attached to their similar achievements in 'lesser' cup competitions in the mid-70s as their first building block, and they delivered their first major trophies for these clubs in close proximity, with Forest's League Cup and league championship and Ipswich's FA Cup coming within a 45-day span in 1978, two years after Southampton's remarkable FA Cup victory. However, it was Clough and Forest who would go on to conquer Europe, while Robson would also bring home a European trophy but would mirror McMenemy in nothing more than near misses in their ambitions to win a league title. McMenemy's on-pitch success after his FA Cup win was more about the football he played, the stars he brought in and their tilts at the title and the double. He would never match the success of his contemporaries in Europe.

It probably reflected Clough's mercurial nature that his greatest success was packed into a whirlwind of three astonishing years. Although he won more, he couldn't maintain his level, stratospheric though it was, in quite the manner of Robson and McMenemy.

Their success meant that each was inevitably in demand throughout these ten years and at club level Robson and McMenemy in particular were highly coveted by some of the top clubs in Europe and were offered several opportunities to leave their smaller parishes in the late 70s and early 80s. Both received offers from the same clubs at the same time when Manchester United and Leeds came calling for one after the other, but they declined every time and remained where they were even when the opportunities had them in two minds or were, as McMenemy put it, 'a tug at the heart strings'. They would both put this down to loyalty to their supportive boards, their desirable autonomy within their clubs and a vision of ongoing potential success where they were. Clough, unsurprisingly, with less interest in the reaction of his directors, played this differently, at times actively courting and teasing his former employers at Derby, where he felt he had unfinished business, but it never came to anything. So, for different reasons they stayed put. Had they not, there would have been no story.

Each was interviewed for the England manager's job at the same time in 1977. Although it was widely anticipated the role would go to one of them, they were passed over in favour of Ron Greenwood, a man less likely to give sleepless nights to FA councillors, which was a frustration for the majority of the England-following public and for Clough himself, who would later reflect, 'So much for the body of opinion that wanted McMenemy installed; so much for those who would've applauded the appointment of Bobby Robson; so much for the opinion polls showing, overwhelmingly, that I was the public's idea of the right man for the job. The entire interview process was just a sop to the public.' There was that element of the anti-establishment about Clough in particular, and perhaps McMenemy to a degree, and the correct assumption that all three were used to running their own show and would intend to do so again led the conservative decision-makers to opt for the more malleable safe pair of hands. One of our subjects ultimately attained the position, one made it as far as assistant manager, and the third is commonly referred to as the best manager England never had.

Through the period of their various successes and greatest competition there was a mutual respect, and they would use each other as both a yardstick and a motivation. In his 1979 book, *The Diary of a Season*, McMenemy notes in his diary after a home defeat by Ipswich and generous comments in victory from Robson, that 'I hold Ipswich as an example of what a smaller club can achieve by sound management. If we can do what they've done in the next five years, I will be satisfied.' They very nearly did.

Of the personal relationships, the closest was that between Clough and McMenemy. While not two peas in a pod, they understood each other and, for the most part until a minor falling-out many years later, held a genuine mutual affection. The fact that McMenemy devotes an entire chapter (entitled 'The Original Special One') of his autobiography to his friend confirms the strength of their relationship, and he opens it saying, 'My friendship with Brian Clough transcended promotions, relegations and the winning and losing of cupties. I was friends with Brian for forty years – more than just ships who passed in the night despite it feeling like that when our clubs were our priority ... we had a lovely relationship.'

Robson's interaction with Clough was different, based more on respect than the closeness shared by Clough and McMenemy. Respect there was, however. Robson wrote, 'Clough was one of my nearest adversaries through much of the 1970s. What a character. He was dogmatic, autocratic, powerful. He deferred to no one.' He also referred to Clough as living on the border between arrogance and confidence, between popularity and unpopularity and that he rejected the norm at every opportunity. From Clough's perspective things changed somewhat when Robson eventually acceded to the throne of England manager, a consequence of the former never being able to accept fully that the role shouldn't have been his own. (He reserved some of his more unhelpful and antagonistic behaviour and comments to the holders of this position throughout his career.) Robson and McMenemy were perhaps a degree closer, with the latter in 1978 referring not only to their friendship but also interestingly to Robson as a man of extreme moods and a bad loser, intended as a compliment but also debunking any misconceptions that Robson was any softer or less competitive than his peers.

In among all the concordance, the clearest distinction was in how they each came to the end of the road – one seemingly getting the timing right and departing with characteristic judicious dignity, going on to burnish his career over another 20 years; one feeling later that he took the wrong option and left when there was more still to achieve – his career rather fizzling out in a manner unbefitting of his talent; one staying too long, which would be a source of lasting regret to himself and his admirers.

Above all, at the end they each left an enduring and valued legacy to their clubs and communities. All were made Freemen of the City and remain a part of the history of these places, earning an enduring gratitude from those players, fans and general public alike to whom they brought a period of unexpected and unprecedented pride and enjoyment that won't pass by in the same way again. Robson once highlighted how much he treasured the words of one of his directors, Murray Sangster, when he finally departed Portman Road: 'I'm really sorry to see you go Bobby. I know you have to, and you're right to leave, but I'd like to thank you because we have seen a decade of football here at Ipswich the likes of which we will never see again.'

This legacy lies in both the 'time of their lives' they created for the inhabitants of these parishes and in the fact that their approaches to management hold value today for those who are wise enough to consider them. Even if what they achieved in football could indeed not be repeated today for a plethora of reasons, the values and principles still work. They were both ahead of their time and ultimately timeless.

Was there some form of elixir behind what they achieved? I'm fascinated by those who can inspire others to exceptional performance and achievements that even the individuals themselves might have doubted were within their compass. I'm interested to learn whether there are commonalties in how a few standout leaders manage this. The sustained success achieved by Pep Guardiola and the transformation of the culture and belief of an underperforming England cricket team under Ben Stokes (another man formed, if not born, in the North East whose inner strength brought him through difficult days) and Brendon McCullum offer clear parallels.

Guardiola said his management has been based on principles he credits to the time he spent learning under Bobby Robson. He may have money at his disposal but so do many others who are unable to match his results. His belief in a simple game of pass and move, and how to communicate to players with a clarity and empathy that begets respect is pure Robson. Stokes's evolution of a winning team with a new spirit and utter belief that no cause is lost, using largely the same personnel who had struggled previously, echoes Clough, as does his placing of trust and consequent building of confidence in the individuals he has identified as the best equipped to execute his philosophy. And when Stokes suggests he likes to select players for his building of teams based on what that player could offer on his very best day, McMenemy's use of the Osgoods, Worthingtons and similar talented rascals comes to mind.

The similarities of method keep coming if you consider Stokes's philosophy. Releasing pressure to unlock talent, gaining rock-solid commitment and building a togetherness that makes players desperate to secure an involvement, through a conspiracy of approach, personality, simplicity, trust and clarity of message ... this bears all the hallmarks of how our managers succeeded. So perhaps, as Marie Antionette believed, there's nothing new other than what has been forgotten. If there *is* a formula, the feats of Clough, Robson and McMenemy, and today of Guardiola and Stokes, suggest it to be a simple and identifiable one: *background and values, a strength of will to survive the toughest moments, establishing respect and authority, valued support networks, a simple playing philosophy, extraordinary gifts for man-management – making better players and better people, creating an unrivalled togetherness, all leading to the building and evolution of successful teams.*

These, allied to recollections of the glory days themselves, the end of the roads, the legacies left to their people and places, and why it all mattered, are the elements that guide us through the pages that follow. This is the story of three men, not identical, but bound together in the way they carried the people and the pride of two cities and one town along with them in a ten-year span never to be forgotten.

And everything can be traced back to, and attributed to, their very beginnings.

Foundations

In the Blood

'For those of us born in the north-east it was
accepted that football would be a vital part of our
lives. Football was in our blood, and we were
helpless victims.'

Lawrie McMenemy

On a good day you can travel from the Teesside town of
Middlesbrough, through the village of Sacriston in County
Durham, and on to Gateshead, Tyne & Wear in about an hour.
Your fuel outlay might be about £1.60 as you covered the 40
miles. Should you choose to take this journey you would be
visiting, whether you were aware of it or not, the birthplaces of
three remarkable football men – three proud sons of the north-
east of England whose characters and beliefs were formed in
that place through their humble upbringings, and whose pride
in this never left them.

'As soon as you can walk in this area you just *have to* love
football.' Alan Shearer, one of its more successful sons, said
this of the North East. My own father, born in Cullercoats,
told stories of what it meant to him to stand with my grandad
on the Gallowgate terraces watching Jackie Milburn and
George Robledo. When the area was dominated by the
uncompromising, physically draining industries of mining and
shipbuilding, the game was the release for the working men
who had little access to, or time or inclination for, any other
pastime that might act as their beacon through the honest

but piteous toil of their week. It gave a depth to their passion bordering on love for the clubs whose role it was to provide them with that respite. There was an obligation on the clubs to give them entertainment as the oxygen for their sacrificial lungs and the success that would gladden their hearts. To them that success was more of a necessity sought with desperation, rather than an occasional happy dividend for their lifelong investment. Once those industries started to disappear, leaving some of the most depressed post-industrial landscapes and stranded communities of good people anywhere in the country, the importance of the clubs became even more pronounced, now as the only vehicles that could offer those communities a sense of pride and a feeling of belonging to set against the sense of decay.

It's perhaps therefore no great surprise that, while there's no monopoly on or geographical stipulation regarding passion for a football club, many would agree that as you proceed south down the country – certainly into the rural shires – the intensity of that attachment and the critical part it plays in so many lives lessens slightly. If you want to take issue with this, I have a reasonable ally in Brian Clough himself, who wrote: 'When I was growing up in the north-east, football was a religion. It was in the blood. Even today, the game generates more passion amongst the folk of that region than anywhere else in the country.'

There's an obvious parallel here with the industrial Scotland of those three kings, Stein, Shankly and Busby, which fed the toughness, the values, the relationships with communities and ultimately the management styles that were the hallmarks of both groups of three. The experiences and hardships in the upbringings that formed the characters and beliefs of the three Glaswegians were precisely those that also moulded McMenemy, Clough and Robson a quarter of a century on. Small wonder that McMenemy should draw the comparison that he did many years later, or that there was a friendship and respect between them all based on a shared understanding, which needed no words for its affirmation. There was a kinship between the North East towns and cities and their near neighbours north of Hadrian's Wall and that brotherhood took on a paternal element as the baton of successful football management was handed on. There's more than coincidence to the fact that the high percentage of successful managers from Scotland over several decades has been replicated – particularly in the 70s and 80s – in those hailing from Tyneside, Wearside, Teesside and County Durham.

Of course, the game has changed and become truly globalised, for better or worse depending on one's opinion. At the time of writing, of the teams occupying the top half of the Premier League, seven out of ten have managers hailing from outside Britain, supplemented by two Englishmen (from the West Midlands and the Home Counties) and one Scot. (Since, in the course of writing this book, so far, 12 managers in the Premier League have lost their jobs, this is bound to be inaccurate by the time it sees the light of day, but I doubt the percentages will have moved much in favour of the home nations in the meantime.)

Consider then ... Bob Paisley, Brian Clough, Bobby Robson, John Barnwell, Lawrie McMenemy, John Neal and Jimmy Adamson. At the end of the 1979/80 season, the heart of our timeframe, of those 11 clubs that finished in the top half of the First Division, seven – *SEVEN* – had managers who were natives of England's north-east. To that you can add the name of Stan Anderson at Bolton further down the table. This not only confirms the breeding ground of top-class coaches that existed in this part of the country, but also a certain comradeship and mutual understanding between these managers of the time, which in turn produced a network of contacts and working relationships that were to prove important to each of them in matters ranging from transfers to personal support and advice.

For Clough, Robson and McMenemy the shared background is as significant as it was for the proud Scotsmen who preceded them. Their lifelong passion for their native area and its people and the values instilled in them by both family and community gave them all a conviction never to forget their roots and many shared beliefs that translated into a similar style of man-management, and that were to prove, in each case, the fundamental pillars of their success. When McMenemy was asked, on a scouting trip back to Newcastle in the late 70s, to divert to do a brief piece with local television, he notes in *The Diary of a Season* that he immediately agreed as 'this is my country, and these are my people'.

In Robson's case, he recalls:

> It was Dad who introduced me to the football addiction which was so rampant in the north-east – he bled black and white – and I became one of the pilgrims who flocked to St James' Park every other Saturday. Those trips provided the inspiration for me. This was the game I loved, on an immense stage, watched by huge legions of Geordies, all willing Newcastle on. This was the passion that was to animate my life.

Robson was to ensure it animated many other lives too, a legacy of which he would be justifiably proud.

Brian Scovell of the *Daily Mail* wrote back in 1979 that most of the 92 Football League club managers were more famed for being sacked than anything else and that the standouts from the few successful ones were McMenemy, Clough, Robson and Paisley. He noted all were 'Geordies' (perhaps not strictly true by the local definition but the point is understood) and people who had a tough upbringing in one of England's less-wealthy areas: 'Their breeding and background seem to have given them the mental capacity to withstand the strains of one of the hardest jobs in sport.' Such inbred resilience would allow each to overcome significant challenges and to impose their authority where it was sorely needed.

That the three men should also be born within three and a half years of each other, in the depressed pre-war decade of the 1930s, is just the first example of the striking accordance of timing that runs through their stories. The spartan but happy nature of their formative years in such a time of austerity meant they each cherished the social fabric of a community, as well as the value of a pound note, and in the end they took pride and satisfaction when reflecting that what they achieved in football with these homespun clubs made its own extremely positive contribution to a similar sense of social cohesion.

Tony Woodcock, one of the strikers Clough inherited at Forest and was within three years turned into the Young Player of the Year, reveals how this belief was something the manager always wanted his players to understand: 'Cloughie was big on saying you had to be *generous*. He didn't mean with money, he meant with your time and your approach to the supporters and the community.' That philosophy, more than just the results and the trophies, is the thing most valued by its beneficiaries.

By the time they were done, each manager had become attached to these places in a way they may not have anticipated, developing an affection and an affinity for the places and their people, the ultimate demonstration being the fact that all three made their long-term homes there even after they departed the clubs themselves and despite the call of their beloved North East. It was not by chance that Sir Bobby's forever home in the Suffolk countryside was named 'Durham House', but he would later say, 'I wouldn't have lived in this town for 33 years if I didn't know what the people of Suffolk were. It's my second home.'

Robson, McMenemy and Clough did indeed become adopted by other places, but they were inspired and driven career-long by what the North East had given them, and the influence that it had on them was the driving force behind what was to come.

Real Life

*'My values stemmed from the family. Anything
I have achieved in my life has been rooted in my
upbringing. Such an upbringing relied heavily
on discipline. What happens in the home affects
you for the rest of your life.'*

Brian Clough

He gave you standards – from how you turned up to
how he expected you to appear on the pitch. He would
tell me every time I left the dressing room to tuck my
bloody shirt in. These may seem small things, but they
were all part of making us what we were. And I believe
Cloughie and Lawrie Mac were the same. If you ever
started to slacken off, Bobby would pull you in and
say, 'You could be working down the fucking mines
… go to Lowestoft, have a look at the trawlers and see
if you fancy being out there.' I heard it was the same
with Lawrie at Southampton with all the dockers and
so on. Bobby reminded you back then that it was a
working-class game – the people coming to support you
had worked hard all week and 'if you aren't prepared to
put a shift in, you're letting them down'.

Russell Osman's recollections of the values that underpinned
the management of the three north-easterners, and how they
were formed, are echoed by the then Southampton midfielder
Steve Williams. He too references the demographic of a good

proportion of their supporter base and that there was a mutual understanding in his manager's relationship with the local dockers, which fed down to their players: 'These are pretty straightforward people and what they expect to see from their players is people breaking their backs and giving one hundred per cent. That was their own experience in life. If you did that, you might eventually get the reward of a bunch of them chanting your name.'

The industrial heartlands of the north-east of England didn't offer the most beatific of landscapes or many homes stocked with creature comforts. Life was real; it was hard. The people who lived it were hard too, which in this context conveys resilience, plain-speaking and no-nonsense folk who suffered no fools and had little truck with airs and graces. These character traits were passed through families and they became every bit as ingrained in Lawrie McMenemy, Brian Clough and Bobby Robson as they were in their parents. But 'hard' does not imply 'uncaring'. There was much love within their homes and families. All three would consider their upbringings happy ones – they had no frame of reference to which they might compare them negatively – and the value they placed on family for the rest of their lives was born of the happiness and mutual support they enjoyed in those years.

Togetherness is a theme that will reoccur later when their players talk of the greatest gift these managers bestowed – an ability to create an environment from less glamorous beginnings, which would foster a group capable of attaining heights transcending the sum of the players' individual talents. This is surely where that ability was incubated. Such communities as these understood that without a hard-work ethic and an inner strength and determination to survive, however tough the circumstances, you would amount to nothing. There was little sympathy for those who would rather moan about their lot than make the very best of it. All three shared career-long disdain for those they considered 'slackers' at their football clubs and there were to be visible consequences of such attitudes in the years ahead.

Bobby Robson experienced life down in the hellhole that was the mine at Langley Park, Durham, as a 15-year-old – something beyond comprehension in today's football world. This chilling baptism and education in real life provided a reference point for him throughout his time in football. He told a story of insisting much later on taking his gentlemen board of directors at Ipswich down a mine in the East Midlands to impress on his employers how fortunate they were. Robson's roots would be a core part of his approach to management, his abhorrence of any players he felt weren't giving their all, or were taking their privileged positions for granted, and his insistence that his own belief in discipline, respect and courtesy, both among themselves and with the wider public, should be adopted and reflected by his players. His empathy with the working-class supporter was born of his experience with his father on the Gallowgate and, as Tony Woodcock said of Clough, he wanted his players to understand it, embrace it and demonstrate it. It was the result of everything he experienced in Langley Park. He remained a man of the people throughout his career – the idea of the current incumbent England manager travelling on the tube and chatting to the public is probably far-fetched, but Robson considered it a privilege.

Ah, the haircuts. Apparently insignificant things mattered, and a constant crusade against the long hair of the youth of the day was just another manifestation of a set of values born of the post-war years for three men who remained short-back-and-sides managers in an era of perms and mullets. Osman confirms that Robson was forever telling players to get their hair cut in the manner of a certain type of deputy headmaster familiar to many of us brought up in those years. Appearance mattered because to them it spoke of the discipline and respect they valued so highly – it was a matter of standards. The former Northern Ireland international, and later manager, Bryan Hamilton, was a key member of Robson's first team that evolved out of the early relegation battles, and he saw at first-hand how his manager's values influenced him and whence they came: 'I think you've touched on something there. I met Bobby's mother and father, and they were the nicest people in the world – solid, high standards, high morals.'

Another rather successful football manager, and another successor to 'the Three Kings' who had also been born and brought up in Glasgow, one Alex Ferguson, reinforces Hamilton's view. Ferguson credits Robson with a huge amount of support and advice during his own climb to the top of the game and got to know the essence of his mentor: 'The foundation he got through his parents, his mining district, and working-class people. Those values never left him.'

Lawrie McMenemy's own character was formed by both his upbringing (and its location in steadfastly working-class Gateshead), and by National Service and his two years spent in the Coldstream Guards. It gave him a strength and a will: 'Gateshead taught me the need to survive, and the Guards taught me how.' This not only had benefits for him as an individual, but ultimately as a manager of men. His army days, he said, taught him discipline but also gave him the confidence to stand in front of a group and coax the best out of them. His former captain Mick Channon remembers the standards upon which he insisted: 'He used to rule by fear with the kids, who were frightened to death of him. It was real army-style discipline. The baths had to be sparkling, the showers immaculately clean and the toilets spotless.'

Clough made famous his 'Mam's' mangle – even giving it its own chapter in his memoirs. The reason this object resided in his own living room for the rest of his life was, he advised, to remind him of whence he came and the sacrifices that had been made on his behalf. For in none of the three households did anything come easy – everything was earned and such matters as respect and doing things the right way were taken as read. Clough's formative years relied heavily on discipline and routine and his father always commanded his respect. Robson's father was a miner, McMenemy's a caretaker, and Clough's was employed in the local sweet factory. Such humble beginnings left each with an understandable taste for the good things in life when they came along (the lack of sunshine holidays in their childhoods may have been the seed that germinated into so many of those mid-season breaks with their teams in later years – particularly beloved of Clough), and also a lasting appreciation of the value of such fruits of success and ultimately a pride that this allowed each of them, in return, to look after their own in the years that followed.

If the location in which they spent their early years played a significant part in building a set of beliefs, the timing was equally relevant. Born in that depressed decade of the 1930s they were perhaps too young to experience Churchill's 'gathering storm' of the approach of war, but each lived as children through the most chilling and brutal conflict in modern history. In an area of important industrial production, not least shipbuilding, living through it is the right description. At times it would have been at their front doors. Those who experienced the dangers and privations of such a period would understandably have a different perspective to today's adolescents about the precious nature of life, stoicism and the value as well as the costs of everyday life. As the child of a mother whose teenage years were those of post-war austerity and rationing – the relief of victory having given way to the realities of its aftermath – I viewed at first-hand the discipline and insistence on good housekeeping and a lack of waste such an experience instilled. It's not too fanciful to suggest this was something that would in time influence how Robson and McMenemy, in particular, managed their clubs' finances with a sense of personal as well as professional responsibility.

So, the building blocks were cemented by an education in life experience, but to translate this to football success would also require an additional grounding in values relating to coaching and management. In this there was to be another shared experience – this time linking McMenemy and Clough specifically. Even those who become renowned for a management style of complete autonomy, and who develop an aura of utter belief, need mentors. In this case it would be one shared mentor. It should come as no surprise that it was another foundation built in the North East. Both men named one man as more responsible than any other for their early coaching development and their ultimate management philosophy. That man was Alan Brown.

Clough was the first to benefit. Not always one to accept the authority of others readily, particularly those he felt weren't up to the mark, Clough remembered how Brown, as manager of Sunderland, broke a holiday to come and find him personally to sign him for the club (the personal touch another tactic that would be employed by all three men in the future to secure the players they most wanted): 'Aware of my new gaffer's strict, straight, and honest reputation, there was immediate respect. It was Alan Brown who taught me about discipline – the value of decent behaviour which was to become the hallmark of my own teams.' It's not hard to see a direct reflection of Clough in Brown when he said of him, 'There were occasions when I was downright scared of the man. He detested shabby clothing and always insisted his players had a trim. I know that I carried his influence and sprinkled it through the game for a long time. Alan Brown was not simply my manager; he was my mentor.'

McMenemy immediately followed Clough under Brown's wing. He and Brown had first connected while the latter was still at Sunderland and McMenemy manager at Bishop Auckland. When Brown departed the North East for Sheffield Wednesday in 1964 his first move was to offer McMenemy a coaching role. The mentorship this was to provide McMenemy was hugely significant to his future story. Alan Brown would change his life. That Brown was from Northumberland was a touchpoint between them that, as with Clough, sparked instant trust and respect. McMenemy remembers him as the strongest personality he had ever known.

What specifically, other than an ahead-of-his-time approach to coaching referenced by McMenemy, did Brown pass on to his charges? A belief that there's no success without discipline was high on the list. 'Discipline is crucial and paramount in working with a large football squad. Alan was very big on discipline – it was part of everything he did. He had the unmistakable air of a leader about him,' said McMenemy. This characteristic would make a huge impression on both him and Clough and build an understanding of the essential component that strong leadership would be in their own personalities and management of men. By contrast, in Bob Harris's view, Robson didn't have a mentor in quite the same way and instead he built his own style, although he was very close to and learned much from Don Howe from their days at West Brom through to their partnership with England many years later.

All these elements – family background, upbringing, their respective early experiences of real life, whether it be down a mine shaft or on the parade grounds of National Service, then their first years in management and their sackings – cultivated a pride, a drive and determination, and a power of personality. The aura each subsequently carried with them was a huge part of their ability to manage. US Army General Norman Schwarzkopf once said, 'Leadership is a potent combination of strategy and character, but if you must be without one, be without the strategy.' Character was something Robson, McMenemy and Clough would display in abundance and develop in their players in due course as one of the most important elements in their effective team building.

In time their power of personality was to become so instantly recognisable and associated with them that they became almost caricatures. But if ever that strength of character was to be tested to its limits, it was on their arrivals at Southampton, Ipswich and Nottingham Forest respectively and what they found waiting for them in the dark days before the dawn.

What their upbringings taught them never left them: a belief in the value of family and support and the importance of community; a determination to remember their roots and a desire that those in their charge as players should appreciate and act upon this too; that trust and honesty were the cornerstones of respect; that discipline and good manners were non-negotiables that cost nothing; that you get nowhere without strength of character, the utmost conviction, a willingness to fight and an unwavering belief in oneself. If their success had a recipe, then these were the base ingredients. Their essential values were established at the outset, were never neglected and would sustain them through, and allow them to outlast, the early tribulations and go on to greatness.

Asleep in the Deep

There's a chapter in Bobby Robson's autobiography entitled 'A Town Awakes', in which he remembered:

> Sleepy Suffolk they called it, but the county woke up alright when we won the FA Cup. It tickles me now to recall the days when I took our supporters to task for being too quiet and undemonstrative at Portman Road. 'Look at the crowd, we've got bloody zombies in here,' I said to Bobby Ferguson. 'We're playing fantastic football – they need to be behind us.' I went public and to their credit they turned the accusation around.

In the old joke, the motorist asks for directions and is offered the helpful advice, 'If I were you, I wouldn't start from here.' That might have resonated with the three managers as each stepped into a job bearing significant challenges. In truth, had these issues not existed, it's unlikely, in the cases of Robson and McMenemy at least, that they would have landed the job ahead of other better-known and perhaps better-qualified candidates in the first place. Ipswich had fallen away significantly from their brief title-winning moment in the sun under Alf Ramsey at the start of the 60s. On Robson's arrival, the former Ipswich manager Jackie Milburn offered the unpromising and ultimately flawed prediction that 'this is a club that's only got one way to go – and that's down'. While Southampton had been just about holding their own in the First Division since promotion in 1966, they were some distance from being the most attractive or sophisticated team – handed the moniker by Bill Shankly of the alehouse brawlers – and were an ageing team dominated by individual personalities who felt they could run things themselves and should be allowed to carry on doing just that. Duncan Hamilton's portrayal of Forest on Clough's arrival was as 'an unappealing, rusting tugboat of a club'. Certainly, all three clubs lacked the infrastructure and finance to compete in any meaningful way or even to dream of doing so.

It wasn't just the clubs that were in something of a torpor. The cities themselves were hardly thriving and their football followers weren't renowned for their passionate and vocal support in the manner of a Manchester United, a Liverpool or even, significantly, a Newcastle United or their north-eastern neighbours. This reticence of the home crowds to create an atmosphere of their own making that could lift their teams was an ongoing battle and concern for each manager. Exasperated at times by what they deemed the sleepy nature of the football communities of Nottingham, Ipswich and Southampton, they often ran the gauntlet of fan displeasure by calling this out and pleading for a higher level of passion closer to that they had grown up experiencing on their home turf.

My discussions with Ipswich and Saints fans suggest that there may have been something cosier and more comfortable in the happiness their clubs' unexpected success brought them than in the desperation for it, which was the natural state of fans of the big-city clubs that were expected to deliver time after time. At Ipswich at least, Tim Smith, a 'Tractor Boy' who moved to Ipswich in 1974 as a two-year-old and left 20 years later as one of the many whose career prospects resided in London rather than his rural hometown, feels the relatively genteel quality of life in Suffolk meant any form of perceived success was fun rather than essential: 'Our fans were having the time of their lives and we had a good atmosphere at

Portman Road, but I would never describe it as hostile. That's not who we were. They would support the team and then head off home to their quaint villages.'

As a Saints fan and resident of Hampshire for 66 years, David Dykes is able to offer a similar opinion with credibility: 'Southerners in my experience are more reserved and fatalistic. Consequently, they had lower expectations of their teams and tended to get less upset. If they lost, it would be "silly old Saints", rather than the end of the world.' If the English have a tendency towards self-deprecation and humour as a defence mechanism, then the English sports fan is often an extension of that, with the southern, provincial fan perhaps the ultimate manifestation. McMenemy tells a story of a lady who, when he suggested people would be dancing in the streets at winning an FA Cup semi-final if the club was up north, replied, 'We are just as proud of you as anyone in the north would be, we just prefer to dance in the kitchen.' Dancing in the streets in Southampton was, in fact, at the time less than a month away.

Initially this perceived apathy was anathema to the three men of the North East, given the blood that coursed through their native region in a way it didn't in their new surroundings, but it remains one of their greatest achievements that, over time, each managed to get the blood pumping in these somnolent football pastures in a way that had never happened before and that allowed those fans to challenge, with good cause for the first time, the truism that real football passion resided in the north-east and north-west of England.

In *The Diary of a Season* McMenemy recalled taking to task the local newspaper for the lack of coverage that even they, as theoretically the most relevant media outlet with the greatest vested interest, gave Saints' semi-final win in the 1979 League Cup, which he felt adduced the small-town outlook in Southampton if a match that took them to Wembley was to be deemed worthy of just eight paragraphs. He was clear that if he didn't continue to fight that attitude, the club would sink back.

But, in time, truly intimidating atmospheres evolved at each of the small, enclosed grounds (as a Saints fan of the era I felt The Dell was probably worth ten points and a couple of extra rounds in the cups to us every season) – something that played its own role in the successes once the ball started rolling and supported Saints' midfielder David Armstrong's assessment of The Dell crowd as the team's 12th man. So, we had our moments. By the time the remarkable Kevin Keegan era was underway the place was jumping. Keegan himself remembered, 'The Dell was full of noise and the tight confines were packed. The atmosphere was crackling, and we fancied our chances against anyone when we were playing at home.' It's an atmosphere I'll personally always remember but it's a description that would have seemed alien just five years earlier. The change was marked but it took time to affect. Although there could be a real cacophony at times, especially in the glory years and when the teams were on the front foot, it was something that was never completely conquered in the eyes of the managers. In truth, their new provincial clubs were never going to be able to match the level of obsession or the noise of 60,000-plus crowds at the major stadiums. But the change in the public's commitment to their football clubs, both inside the ground and in the wider community, was generated as much by the personalities and exhortations of the managers as by results.

The irony may not have been lost on Robson and McMenemy in particular that their respective crowds had no trouble finding their voices when chanting for them to be relieved of their duties in the early days. Both had arrived with minimal reputations as managers and as choices that scarcely got the hearts of the supporters racing, with sackings on their CVs at clubs even further down the league ladder. Things ran far from smoothly at first. A Saints season-ticket holder at the time of McMenemy's appointment, David Dykes recalls, 'The fans were distinctly underwhelmed. He had to deal with a groundswell of anti-McMenemy feeling from the fans. I suppose the problem was he couldn't use his undoubted man-management skills on *them*.'

Their ultimate longevity in their roles and the time they were given to build success were by no means givens over these first few seasons, and it's impossible to envisage them surviving today's maelstrom of managerial comings and goings. The fans can be thankful that the managers' employers had a clearer vision and greater strength and resolve than many of them did themselves. The very real risk that the glory of the next ten years might not have happened at all is a sobering thought for those whose lives it changed. The most obvious relatively modern, and probably last, parallel to their experience would be that of Alex Ferguson at Manchester United. Early struggles, fan dissent, a precarious position but a board that held its nerve and maintained its support, followed by a period of unprecedented success – with what happened to that club following his departure being a salutary lesson for those in charge of clubs today, but one it appears that has rarely been heeded.

Robson was feeling his way on arrival and wasn't universally welcomed even in his own dressing room, which may be understandable given even he felt that he didn't have any real credibility as a manager. His first two seasons (1969/70 and 1970/71) gave precious little indication of the imminent turnaround, with 18th and 19th finishes indicative of two uncomfortable relegation battles. For the fans who had begun the decade with a league championship win, under a man who would go on to win a World Cup, these efforts were hardly cause for satisfaction or optimism. The following season saw something of an improvement but 13th was no great shakes either. It did, however, include the arrival of centre-half Allan Hunter from Blackburn in its second month and, before the start of the next, a young former apprentice called Kevin Beattie would be added to the first-team squad. Few could anticipate it then but today they're considered the two most critical parts of the jigsaw Robson was beginning to piece together. Then 1972/73 would produce the first evidence of the turning of the tide, but for now that seemed a long way beyond the Suffolk coastline.

Robson may have flirted with relegation, but McMenemy went one better and nailed it within six months (or 12 depending upon your view of his initial 'manager designate' title and its associated level of responsibility, or blame), from a position of sixth place in November. If that was a shock to McMenemy, it wasn't well received by his senior pros either and it hardly helped his struggle to earn early respect and credibility. Mick Channon was livid, considering McMenemy tactically inept at that stage and concerned about the impact Second Division football would have on his two-year-old England career. (The irony being that Channon's final international cap would come within a month of the big-club move he'd been seeking ever since, which therefore had the opposite effect to that he had imagined it would.)

If it was anticipated that this would be a short-lived stay in the second tier, that would prove overly optimistic across the following four seasons, which is the time it took McMenemy to right the wrong. Even with a board of directors not given to managerial change, having employed the previous incumbent for 18 years and remained fully behind their man, it's doubtful such results would have kept McMenemy in a job, big personality or not, were it not for the small matter of something called the FA Cup two years on. However, 1974/75 regularly had him suffering catcalls from dressing room to dugout, not least because his first solution to the club's problems had been to eject the fans' favourite, Terry Paine.

The manager found himself confronted with the same senior pro problem that had greeted Robson at Ipswich, and he was equally convinced that it had to be addressed. With hindsight it was a brave, necessary and wise decision but at the time he desperately needed an immediate promotion to assuage the unrest and it wasn't to be forthcoming. There was, however, one moment in his first year that was eye-catching enough to suggest McMenemy might have something about him: the transfer of Peter Osgood from Chelsea and the King's Road to Southampton marked the first and, in the manager's view, most important of the big names he would convince to come to the club and then help to extract their talent over the years ahead. It would prove a significant piece of business.

Even Clough took some time to produce his Svengali act at the City Ground. 'In the first six months he was feeling his way,' remembers Tony Woodcock. He may have had money in the bank after his Leeds experience, sacked after 44 tempestuous days of poor results and player mutiny, but his credibility account was in danger of slipping into the red. The disaster at Leeds had been played out in the full glare of the media in a manner that McMenemy and Robson didn't have to suffer. Added to an impetuous walkout at Derby and an incongruous trip to Third Division Brighton, which had the feel of an Indian summer holiday, he was no longer everyone's first choice (even Forest's board had some dissenters with significant doubts about his appointment at the turn of the year). In the infamous Yorkshire Television interview in which Clough and Don Revie sat together in the same studio shortly after Clough's Leeds sacking, and Clough once again reinforced his reputation for searing honesty, host Austin Mitchell asked Clough straight out, 'Who's going to touch you with a barge pole?' It was a question crossing many minds, perhaps even that of Clough himself. Whisper it, but had the big mouth, to use his own words, 'shot it'?

And while not suffering the early opprobrium of his supporters in the way of Robson and McMenemy, there was another irritant and a driving force for Clough to prove himself once more. Four months after he arrived at his second East Midlands club in the middle reaches of the Second Division, he saw his successor at Derby, Dave Mackay, lead them to their second league championship in four years. The first had been Clough's and he always felt he had unfinished business at Derby, his stage-managed high-noon moment with the board there not having ended as he had anticipated or desired. To see the club not only manage without him but repeat his success was a dagger he saw before him constantly until he was able to take his new club's achievements past those of his old one. It made success at Forest essential to him rather than merely desirable.

At that 'rusting tugboat of a club', he found several players not up to it, a few youngsters in whom few others could see any great potential – hidden to all but the eye of the nonpareil Clough and his shrewd footballing partner Peter Taylor – and a good quotient of journeymen who seemed happy with a footballing life of leisure, accompanied by a pint and a fag. Those journeymen would of course in many cases go on to win two European Cups, but at the time such a thing was a preposterous notion. At the start of 1975 nobody saw anything but mediocrity in the lot of them. While 16th in the Second Division in 1974/75 may have been something he could partially disown, given he turned up halfway through the season, he had arrived with Forest in 13th and won only one of his first 12 matches, which hardly suggests an immediate impact. Eighth in his first full season was an improvement but hardly in the realms of Clough magic, and it certainly didn't appear to be presaging the conquering of Europe.

These sleepy clubs were going to be difficult to turn around. The managers' early struggles also left them well aware that if they couldn't affect such a change in direction, their careers were likely to be the casualties. This was the moment when those deeply ingrained values and the strength imbued by their upbringings and personalities would have to make the difference. They could easily have folded. Each one in their own way came to the same conclusion … if they were going to do this, they were going to do it their way. It was time to show who was boss.

My Way

'Through it all when there was doubt, I ate it up and spit it out, I faced it all and I stood tall and did it my way.'

Paul Anka, 'My Way'

Few of those self-important, self-proclaimed 'bibles' of management instruction that seem to have landed like a plague on train station bookshelves today are likely to include a fistfight with one's senior employees as one of their top ten recommended techniques for the modern business manager. Nor was one such dust-up Bobby Robson's proudest moment. It was, however, a critical one in his career, establishing an authority once fragile but never again to be challenged. The time had come to stand and deliver.

The location, timing and manner of their upbringings not only built within the three managers an utter belief in their ability to achieve success through the strict application of discipline, respect and trust, but also fostered a conviction that they must establish that authority and gain a domination of their football clubs rare to the point of non-existent in today's game. Clough insisted many years later that even in the modern game the manager has to be the boss, suggesting that you have to be a dictator or you haven't got a chance.

Aldous Huxley, a man whose childhood nickname of 'Ogre' perhaps suggested more of a similarity to Clough than did his pacifism, wrote: 'Those who believe they are exclusively in the right are generally those who achieve something.' As a pointer to one of Clough, McMenemy and Robson's key characteristics, this could scarcely be bettered. Whether it was simply coincidence that they shared a love of Frank Sinatra and played his music more than any other, or whether the words of his most famous curtain call had a genuine impact, McMenemy, Robson and Clough all understood they *had* to do it 'my way'.

If what doesn't kill you does indeed make you stronger and character is built in adversity, the successes of 1975–1985 undoubtedly stood on the shoulders of what came before. McMenemy and Robson talk of the humiliation of sackings at Doncaster and Fulham respectively – of the sense of having let down those close to them and that it was a feeling they were sure never to forget. Both were in the throes of trying to establish a reputation that might build a career and at these moments it was hard not to worry whether that had just vanished on the wind. Clough's own dismissal at Leeds United was different in that he came and went at Elland Road with his CV already established through championship-winning success. Nonetheless, it was a humiliation and not something from which the majority expected him to recover. But they all took learnings and a renewed determination from these experiences that were to have huge influence on the years ahead. Robson reasoned, to himself as much as anyone, that few people get to the top unless they've had it rough at some stage and he later acknowledged the role those years would have in his ultimate success: 'It's a tough world out there and if you aren't tough yourself you won't survive or get to where you want to be.'

Leeds gave Clough something more immediate and measurable – what he termed 'fuck-you money'. This granted him a financial security that allowed him to shelve any self-doubt and continue to manage on his own unique terms – something that was to benefit Nottingham Forest and its supporters to an astonishing degree.

Others may have lost some faith in Clough's ability, but that wasn't something to which he was often prone, and he knew what he had to do as a result of his recent past: 'From the moment I left Leeds some club was going to benefit from Brian Clough's belief in his own ability and the sure knowledge I could do the job precisely the way I wanted – on my own terms.' Totalitarianism was going to be fundamental, whatever it might take to achieve it.

One of the benefits of joining smaller provincial clubs was that the opportunity to run the whole show from top to bottom was a perfect fit for the characters involved. Bob Harris would meet with Robson regularly at Portman Road in his professional capacity and saw for himself that 'everything to do with Ipswich, Bobby ran'. Robson said on his arrival, 'This is a club which will allow me to manage and is prepared to give me that chance.' By 1978 he had taken full advantage of that opportunity as his former club press officer, Mel Henderson, noted: 'Actually, Bobby Robson *was* the club. Bobby was first into the office in the morning and was the one who turned off the lights in the evening … he made it his business to get involved in just about everything.'

Such control may have meant long hours – perhaps less so for Clough who, as ever, achieved the same result via his own inimitable methods – but it allowed them to execute their plans in exactly the way they wanted and to build the clubs in their own image. This was not something that those managing at the powerhouse clubs of the time were ever going to be afforded, regardless of the strength of their personalities, as Clough had discovered at Leeds, and they understood the value of the power they could wield – another factor they considered in their assessment of the plusses and minuses of staying where they were. In fact, Clough only moved to Leeds after Robson had turned down the apparently plum job. Part of the reason was, as Robson explained, 'I had a high-calibre team and a good quality of life. I had the best employment conditions, and I was king of my domain.' McMenemy would cite similar feelings and reasons when turning down job offers in the future too, not least from Manchester United.

This effective dictatorship wasn't handed to them on a silver platter, albeit in the case of Clough his prior success and famed personality did afford him a greater level of immediate power. Nor would it have happened at any of the respective clubs without their power of personality. Clough's was well established in advance, and he controlled his fiefdom straight away through a combination of fear and unpredictability. He made himself, in the words of his biographer Duncan Hamilton, 'the axis on which the club always turned'. Tony Woodcock was one of those meandering along at the club when Clough arrived and remembers, 'He came through the doors and it was like a whirlwind and we all thought, "What's going to happen here?" You know something's going to happen. Brian was certainly a big personality and you had to be able to look after yourself.'

Clough wasn't greeted by the player-power issues common to Robson and McMenemy. In both those cases there was a clear issue with established stars, used to getting their own way, and who probably saw a vested interest in undermining the new, unproven boss. The Roman poet Persius suggested that disease should be confronted at its onset, and had either manager not had the foresight, courage and strength to address these particular cancers straight away they could scarcely have become the dominant presences of the future. Establishing authority was going to be a more challenging matter at Ipswich and Southampton. At the time the political landscape encouraged a strong suspicion that the unions, not the government, were running the country, the Conservatives having lost the battle for control. It wasn't an outcome any of our managers could afford to repeat as they looked to wrest power from their own set of shop stewards.

At Portman Road, Robson was conscious that he was a young manager with no reputation, no credibility, no CV, and he had wondered who was ever going to employ him. It was against this background that he encountered two senior players in Tommy Carroll and Bill Baxter. Carroll was demanding terms for a new contract, which Ipswich couldn't afford, and he became truculent and disobedient at the training ground.

Baxter, Carroll's fellow agent provocateur, as Robson considered him, challenged the manager – then just two seasons into his tenure – on the training pitch. As captain, and having been at the club for years, not to mention being the type of tough Scotsman many clubs possessed as their beating heart at that time, Baxter was testing Robson's authority – a critical moment for the latter. Stand and deliver time. Robson duly sent him away and dropped him. This is when he and the two players came to blows, with Robson's valued number two, Cyril Lea, evening up the numbers.

It was as seminal a moment as McMenemy was to face on arrival at his own club and Robson was in no doubt as to its importance: 'To lose a power struggle with a tough, senior player might have been fatal to my prospects of establishing the respect of my squad.' In fact, the incident led directly to the emergence of that very respect, with the rest of the squad siding with their young manager. He was never again to be challenged in such a way and the players understood that Mr Robson was a tougher case than many may have assumed. Robson also saw it as further evidence that he was going to be backed by his chairman all the way. Although they were two of the club's better players and more valuable assets, 'Mr John', the legendary chairman of the club John Cobbold, instructed Robson to get shot of them straight away. Bryan Hamilton also recalls the significance: 'From that point he was allowed the time to do what he was going to do over the next ten years.' Loyalty and respect were to be two of the core ingredients in how all three men ran their own show. In one act Robson had established both.

In McMenemy's case at Southampton the problems were both general – what he considered a shocking lack of discipline at the club – and specific in the person of his inherited club captain, Terry Paine, who bestrode the club as a colossus. Paine's status at Saints was well established and his authority on the pitch and in the dressing room unquestioned. What's more, he had enjoyed a career-long and personally close relationship with McMenemy's predecessor Ted Bates and was, alongside Ted, considered 'Mr Southampton'. Bates's continued role at the club after McMenemy's arrival gave the latter another challenge, initially at least. Centre-half at the club at the time Paul Bennett felt that 'Lawrie spent a lot of time trying to prove he was in charge, rather than in-waiting. He hated the manager designate title which didn't sit well with his ego or help his authority.'

A season-ticket holder in those embryonic early days, David Dykes confirms there were two things in particular that made things difficult for the manager in the eyes of the fans. 'One – he replaced Ted Bates and it felt to us like nobody knew who was running the side. The other – he instigated the moving on of Terry Paine.' The rub being that if you're going to make such a brave decision, you had better not hang about in backing it up with some success because 'a lot of old-school supporters had watched Paine for the best part of 20 years; who was this bloke who hadn't played the game to come in and get shot of their legend?'

Paine was certainly no wallflower. He had built up his power base at the club over many years and was not, it seemed, ready to cede hegemony to this outsider without what he considered good reason, in much the same way as Baxter at Ipswich a couple of years before him. Although conjecture, players at the club at the time such as Mick Channon, Paul Bennett and Hughie Fisher all feel it was likely that Paine had considered the manager's office should have been his for the taking on Bates's eventual retirement, which was not to be.

McMenemy was taken aback on his arrival at The Dell by what he considered the laissez-faire attitude to discipline and drinking, which he felt bordered on the bizarre. These were the 'alehouse brawlers' of Bill Shankly's disapproving phrase. McMenemy thoroughly disapproved too and realised the job he had at hand.

He was, of course, well aware of Paine's quality and standing and had assumed he would be his on-field champion. He was quickly forced to reassess. It became apparent to him, firstly via word of mouth, then by the evidence of his own eyes and ears, that Paine was undermining whatever he was trying to build. In McMenemy's view, Paine was the most obvious example of those who refused to give credibility to anyone who hadn't played the game at the highest level. Ultimately, McMenemy felt Paine and the wider player attitudes at the club were significant factors in the relegation he had to endure six months into his tenure – something he acknowledged left him feeling 'physically sick – a total failure'. He reflected at the season's end that he had shown his players too much respect, not least Paine, and that his management hadn't been in tune with what had brought him his success and reputation up to that point and secured him the job in the first place – namely discipline on and off the pitch, a clear way of playing and effective man-management.

Matters came to a head at an unscheduled player-instigated meeting that was clearly not designed to put the seal of approval on their manager's methods and authority. It was, McMenemy was to reflect, the biggest single moment in his management career and from then on he was going to do it his way. With that, at the end of his first season Paine was gone. A courageous move given the opprobrium this was going to generate from supporters who saw Paine as one of the few stars they could cling to, and who duly articulated this through those boos as the manager walked the cinder track to and from the home dugout in the year that followed. But it was his own *High Noon* moment, equivalent to Robson's, without which the 'my way' route to success would have been stillborn.

Again, there's a parallel with the most successful club manager of the last 30 years. After their respective departures from Ipswich and Southampton, Robson and McMenemy would have empathised with the situation of United's Alex Ferguson, another manager who had to take the tough and unpopular decisions before embarking on unparalleled success, addressing a culture at his club that was a clear barrier to success, shipping out fan favourites (in his case the likes of Paul McGrath and Norman Whiteside) regardless of their on-field class and establishing his own brand of discipline and authority. His board also backed him to make those unpopular decisions, to trust his judgement of when it was the right time to move players on and build again and, in Ferguson's case, by the time he came to do the same thing with Ince, Keane and then Beckham, his position was impregnable. The Scot's journey travelled a similar road to the one these managers had been down before him ... and his didn't turn out too badly either.

A full-back and key component of the 1984 Saints side, Mark Dennis wasn't renowned as an easy character to manage, some way from a well-behaved shrinking violet, but he retains immense respect for his manager's strength of character and saw parallels too. In *Southampton's Cult Heroes*, an anthology of the club's most revered players over the years by journalist Jeremy Wilson, Dennis remembered with some admiration, 'Very few people crossed him and if you did cross him your days were usually finished at the club. He was very similar to Brian Clough in that regard.'

As we'll discover when considering the respective approaches to team building and handling players with a certain reputation, they saw a clear distinction, articulated by McMenemy, between *rascals* and *villains*. The former they saw as players whose approach to life and football might be in the bon viveur category but who, if managed well, would be positive influences at the club on and off the pitch; villains by contrast were the terrorists who would bring little but trouble. In rascals they were willing to place their trust; with villains there was no such understanding. Trust was going to be critical. The villains had to go.

Interviewed for this book, the man who captained McMenemy's 1976 FA Cup-winning team, Peter Rodrigues, said the first thing that came to mind for him was the discipline that went hand in hand with building that trust and it wasn't just his own manager in whom he saw this quality. Of Clough he said, 'I would love to have played for that man. At one stage I was considering going into the army and I would have loved his discipline.' It's not uncommon to hear players who never played under Clough saying they wished that they had – perhaps the greatest nod of all to his reputation for man-management and his mystique. In *Cult Heroes* Jeremy Wilson suggests that McMenemy could be superb with people, but it would be 'hard to imagine him ever compromising a strongly held view in the interests of diplomacy'. Consider that contention as applicable to all three.

Whatever their varied management track records and reputations on arrival, that power of personality they shared was also to be vital in acquiring full control, their aura affording them real personal impact. That inner steel 'in the blood' would come across to all those who dealt with them and, in addition to allowing them to run their clubs as dictators, it consistently showed itself in an ability to get more out of players than others could. Terry Butcher says of Robson, 'He was tough because he wanted you to be the best you could be. He definitely just had this aura about him.' It's something apparent in the make-up of many a successful leader of men and developer of talent. John McGovern followed Clough to three different clubs and is clear where his ultimate loyalty lay: 'It could've been any club – I'm working for the man himself.'

Clough was mercurial in spinning straw into gold as a footballing Rumpelstiltskin. McMenemy had his moral and physical strength, which demanded respect – you might disagree with Lawrie, but you were unlikely to proceed far if the debate became physical.

Mick Channon may have been a confident and outspoken leader in Saints' dressing room, unconvinced by McMenemy's footballing credibility when he arrived, but he's clear that nobody post-Terry Paine disrespected him. He refers to his manager's commanding but courteous ex-guardsman demeanour and articulate way with words. It was to prove an effective combination:

> Lawrie was sharp. He could put you down in front of anybody with a one-liner, humorous or not – and he could be very funny – or make you feel a million dollars. That's how in the end he got the best out of people. He used his wits to establish his authority. He also had an instinct to survive which I reckon came from his guardsman background. He was nobody's fool.

This was Channon's respectful assessment despite Paine being his close mate at the time, whose departure suggested to him that the club and McMenemy were going nowhere fast. Both Channon and his erstwhile team-mate Nick Holmes identify that, critically in their view in the circumstances, the manager was a quick learner. Very little in his interaction with others passed him by or was discarded in planning his future strategy.

Bobby Robson's personality came across differently and could be misconstrued. One former player (although tellingly not one of his own), who shall remain anonymous, suggested to me that in his opinion 'Bobby Robson had all the personality of a paper bag'. Nobody who actually played under Robson would agree with that assessment. Although Robson may not have so obviously been a self-promoter in the manner of Clough and McMenemy, he did have that intangible something. Bryan Hamilton remembers: 'When things were going well, he had a real swagger. We called it his John Wayne roll,' and one of his most feted former players, Alan Shearer, is clear: 'Bobby was a showman.' He was described by no less a disciple than Pep Guardiola as 'one of the nicest people I have ever met in my life' – certainly not a description that was universally applied to Clough by his professional charges. True, Bobby, in the main, personified a relative calm, trust and loyalty. But it's as well to beware stereotypes and to challenge caricatures. Looking past the standard perceptions perhaps throws a brighter light upon their remarkable achievements.

Robson wouldn't have achieved what he did in the game purely by playing the nice guy, and although his wife Elsie referred to a tenderness in him she also saw an immense drive. Although he's recalled with real affection by almost all who played under him, Gary Lineker is of the opinion that 'yes, he was likeable but, boy, he had an edge'. Allan Hunter agrees: 'He was tough, very tough, when he needed to be.' In the same conversation Russell Osman added, 'No mistake, like Cloughie and Lawrie, Bobby was the same – if there was a square-up with the players Bobby would go nose-to-nose. It was "if you want to make an issue of it, let's go". And that's a reflection of their background.' Robson was indeed personable and convivial, but he was also serious – those who mistook his courteous manner for a lack of steel would soon be disillusioned.

The same misconception could be applied to Clough but in reverse – he may often have been abrasive to the point of insulting, but he was also capable of the most generous acts of spirit when the mood took him. A 'Cloughism', typical of his everlasting ability to mix acerbic rudeness and crass insensitivity with moments of empathy, is referred to by

McMenemy in a way that suggests it mattered to him deeply. After Clough's Forest had defeated Southampton in a pulsating League Cup Final at Wembley in 1979, without warning he took his friend's hand and insisted he accompany him up to the royal box – a complete breach of the accepted protocol and one that left the Southampton manager feeling embarrassed at the time, but warmly appreciative ever after.

Hughie Fisher, one of the players McMenemy valued most in his early Saints teams and widely regarded as one of the nicest men to pull on a shirt, offered me another example:

> In the 1971/72 season I broke my leg badly and was out a long time. My first game back was the first of the following season against Cloughie's league champions, Derby. He had no need to – I didn't even know he remembered my injury – but before the game he came over to me and said, 'All the very best of luck young man.' It stuck with me. I would love to have played for that man.

This fondness for the unpredictable and the ability to blow hot and cold kept players 'at it' and desperate to be on the right side of Clough's moods, just as Channon suggests was the case with McMenemy, and it was key to the effectiveness of their motivational tactics.

The media – as it is now and was then – played a significant role in both the survival and then the increasing authority of Robson and McMenemy in particular. David Dykes makes a salient point when considering how the latter managed to ride out the fan approbation in a way he wouldn't today: 'We didn't have social media then – you might get a disgruntled letter to *The Echo* – and as a result there was no platform for a real groundswell because such things just didn't exist. I never really knew what the man on the street was thinking … I only knew what my dad was thinking.' Not only was the less all-consuming media of their day probably a factor in their survival, but all three understood just how the media worked in the 70s and in time used it skilfully to build the profile of clubs the press had previously deemed unnewsworthy.

This was a tactic Clough first honed at Hartlepool. He never missed a chance to get the media there with cameras and notebooks. In effect they were establishing their authority not just within their clubs but with the people who reported on them. Each felt at times that their clubs' feats weren't getting the credit or the column inches they deserved from the press, and they would call them out on it. McMenemy was particularly irritated, as was apparent in part of his post-match interview with a wrong-footed Jimmy Hill, having just won the FA Cup. In the run-up to that final he felt all the attention was on Manchester United and that Saints surprised the press because 'they don't see us enough. They watch the First Division. I was very surprised some of them didn't even ring me this week. No, I'm serious Jim.'

Addressing this lack of standing was one of the benefits that could be reaped from their own significant media profiles and specifically their television work. Clough had been an old hand at this for many years prior to coming to Forest, taking his celebrity to another level by appearances on *Parkinson* and indirect appearances as one of the impressionist's most memorable turns on *The Mike Yarwood Show*. People who had little idea about football certainly had an idea about Brian Clough. Clough of course milked it because he fully understood that with profile came power. He was much loved by the media given he appeared to be the living embodiment of the singer Joan Baez's rhetorical question, 'I've never had a humble opinion. If you've got an opinion, why be humble about it?', which could serve as the epitaph to his entire management career.

McMenemy's case was rather more unusual. For a manager who had spent less than a year at a First Division club (and suffered relegation), and previously only held positions at the likes of Doncaster and Grimsby that could hardly be considered high-profile, to be recruited to the national television 1974 World Cup panel of experts was akin to Gary Johnson or Phil Parkinson being asked to sit alongside Gary Lineker to present the tournament today.

I asked Mick Channon what the players made of it and how on earth he had got the gig: 'Because he was great copy. He was a huge character, Lawrie, regardless of his playing or managing background. Great for TV.' As a fan, David Dykes's memory supports this view: 'I think he gave a couple of post-match interviews early on at Saints where he had the sharp line, the quick retort, and he made people laugh. So, he got noticed and the cameras seemed to like him.' The sense that McMenemy's personality took him to certain places somewhat ahead of his time is reflected in Dykes's reaction to him being interviewed for the England job in 1977: 'I remember when Revie resigned and they interviewed Clough, Robson and Lawrie and I thought, "Hang on, what's McMenemy doing in there? He's there because of World Cup panels, not because he's a great manager." Yes, okay, the FA Cup in 76 … but he still wasn't even a First Division manager. He was far more valid in 82.'

Gradually, the three were using this level of personal impact to survive, to establish authority and to turn the tide. It was not, however, something they could have managed alone.

'A Pint for Mr Osman'

'Everyone needs that support around them.
There's a general consensus amongst the old
players when we get together that the most
influential person who shaped the future of the
club was John Cobbold. Bobby couldn't have done
it without him.'

Bryan Hamilton

'We'll support you ever more' goes the terrace song beloved of 1970s football crowds. The courage and loyalty of their boards of directors, the strength and encouragement of their close families, and the building of high-class support staffs, for all their ultimate dominance of their clubs and the successes that followed, without any one of these three pillars of support what happened wouldn't have happened.

For Robson and McMenemy the early tribulations were eased by the support of boards of directors of an almost identical character. While it might be impossible to bracket anyone as 'identical' to the inimitable John Cobbold at Ipswich, both men refer to special relationships with gentlemen directors and acknowledge that the obligation and desire they felt to return their loyalty was a deciding factor in their rejections of the frequent advances from other chairmen.

It's highly doubtful that Clough ever referred to any of his own directors as 'gentlemen' retaining as he did a somewhat uncharitable view of their perceived motives and machinations.

His career is a story of spectacular fallouts that dictated his direction of travel, some of which he came to regret forever. He was not unaware of the benefits McMenemy and Robson enjoyed with their boards, suggesting that the Cobbolds at Ipswich headed the best board of directors in football. He did value the honourable exceptions in his career that were Mike Bamber at Brighton, although the always temporary-feeling nature of Clough's sojourn there rather reduces the relevance of that happy relationship, and more importantly Stuart Dryden at Nottingham Forest. He would later pay Dryden the compliment that without his support the success he achieved at Forest wouldn't have been possible, and remembered him as a good loyal man and the best of friends.

But the fact remains that while Robson and McMenemy developed working relationships closer to friendships, for all the success and the trophies, Clough never wanted, or encouraged, such warmth in his own boardroom other than the friendship with Dryden – probably as a man who often fed on conflict and a sense of bloody-minded injustice to fuel his success. Although an authoritarian himself, he never lost that inherent distrust of the authority of others, incubated at an early stage in his career and probably rubber-stamped most significantly by his disdainful rejection by the FA. Peter Taylor once suggested, admittedly at a time when he had an axe to grind, that Clough was not as self-assured as he liked people to think, and that the bombast was a defence mechanism against this. The contempt for board members who were prepared to challenge him in any way, from Sam Longson at Derby to Derek Pavis at Forest, might give this credence. Duncan Hamilton suggested of Clough that anybody at his own club who interfered or was willing to question him on his transfer record or other decisions was considered to be insolent.

If Clough's experience with directors wasn't in accordance with that of his two peers, nor did it need to be in quite the same way. His past achievements and his profile encouraged the sense that he was doing Nottingham Forest a favour in taking over when in reality it was the other way round. Firstly, this meant that he was likely to be afforded plenty of time to make his mark, the odds of his running out of patience before his employers did being quite high; secondly, given some of his treatment of directors in previous roles and his habit of publicly belittling the role of such people, it would have been understandable if some of his new board were at least a little apprehensive. He consequently felt less in need of the support so valued by McMenemy and Robson.

In contrast to Clough's reluctance to apportion much credit further up the chain, McMenemy is in no doubt as to how fortunate he was to be working at Southampton. Those early disappointments, the power struggle with Paine and the application of the discipline needed to change the culture of the club could easily have resulted in a short tenure, and it required the firm and public support of those who had hired him, without which he couldn't have prevailed. The directors understood there were issues to address at the club and they wanted to back their man in undertaking that job. They would stand by him, having no truck with fan dissent. In general, the fan power that so regularly determines the futures of managers today, particularly in the Premier League, wasn't as influential then, even if it wasn't exactly a plus point.

The Saints' directors had what now appears to be an old-fashioned belief that there was a certain way of conducting business and managing those they employed with a duty of care. Resorting to the excuse so commonly trotted out today that the manager had 'lost the dressing room' would have been unthinkable to them. In those days you could lose the dressing room and the supporters, for a while at least, as long as you didn't lose those who had employed you. Having achieved only that relegation, albeit with some mitigating circumstances, in his first season in charge McMenemy was at his lowest ebb and by no means sure he would be given another chance to build his vision of the future. That he was, supported by his gentlemen directors George Reader and Sir George Meyrick, changed Southampton – the club and the city – over the next ten years. McMenemy recalls their civilised attitude being very different to many of those in charge at bigger city clubs at the time. In a carbon copy of the John Cobbold philosophy at Ipswich they gave their appointed man the time and freedom from interference to organise every aspect of the club as he saw fit. Their reward would come with the FA Cup victory (which McMenemy indicated to them, as they looked on from their seats in the Wembley stands, was 'for you' after the cup had been presented, 'because they had really looked after me and stood by me') and then with promotion and the years of fun that followed. McMenemy understood they had given him time to recover, to reinvent the club and take it forward. He knew he would have to start virtually from scratch.

The closest relationship between manager and board, however, was that of Robson at Ipswich. While McMenemy needed that initial support, he delivered an unfathomable FA Cup triumph within three years, which completely changed the dynamic; Clough produced a league championship title within the same timeframe. After three years at Ipswich, Robson was only just beginning to affect the turnaround, and for all the positive signs of top-four finishes in the league and unprecedented European adventures, he had to wait nine years for his first major trophy. He was in the greatest need of staunch backing and the durability of that support. He was to get it in a way for which he would be forever grateful, and the town of Ipswich should be too.

If George Reader and his colleagues on the south coast were indeed 'civilised', it's a moot point whether that precise adjective could be applied to the legendary brothers who ran the show at Portman Road, John and Patrick Cobbold. The club has always been associated in fans' minds with the world of agriculture, hence the 'Tractor Boys' nickname. Perhaps it was appropriate that the language used by their chairman in particular was of the sort that often goes hand in hand with that industry. But there was also an aristocratic air to the former public schoolboys that embellished their colourful characters. Russell Osman was born in Derby, a Derby supporter through Clough's tempestuous and successful time at that club, and he recalls Robson telling Clough that 'the difference in our chairmen is that I've got John Cobbold and you've got Sam Longson. Your chairman swears like a farmer; at least my chairman swears like a gentleman.'

Mr John and Mr Pat, as they were affectionally and reverentially known by all at the club (and from talking to those players who contributed to this book, they still are), were something else – perhaps the first and last of the football directors who were even more entertaining than their players. Mr John in particular is remembered by his employees as a true eccentric. The fact that the business he and his brother owned, which was the financial lifeblood of the club, was a local brewery may help explain their view that the football was merely an excuse for regular alcohol-fuelled celebrations, regardless of results. Robson spoke of them with huge affection and cherished the support they gave him without which he would never have had the chance to impact the future so dramatically. He recalled his chairman as 'an old Etonian with a stammer, a fondness for strong drink, and a brilliant sense of the absurd'. He adored Mr John and his Corinthian approach to those two imposters, triumph and disaster – namely that a bottle of champagne would be opened to celebrate a victory, while a loss would require someone to uncork a far greater number. With the Cobbolds there was rarely any risk of deficiency in refreshment.

Russell Osman tells two tales that epitomise their unusual approach and their insistence on enjoyment as the raison d'être not only for the running of their football club but for life itself:

The chairman would always hold his pre-season party on the Thursday night before the first home game of the season – just after Bobby had given his annual lecture on standards and the rule of no drinking from Thursday onwards before a game. Player attendance at the party was fully expected, or pretty much compulsory, and the last player standing had to put Mr John to bed and lock up ... although he did still have a habit of coming back down in his pyjamas.

According to Osman, Mr Pat also believed in the strict implementation of this philosophy:

> We were playing Arsenal at Portman Road and at about one o'clock I was in the lounge while Bobby and some of the players were finishing their pre-match meal. In the restaurant nearby Mr Pat was at the end of the bar and shouted, 'Osman, come and have a fucking drink.' I said, 'Mr Pat, the manager's in the next room and he'll go berserk if he sees me drinking.' 'Osman, you are an employee of this club – at the moment – and so is Mr Robson. I'm the fucking chairman and if I say have a fucking drink, you have a fucking drink.' 'Okay, I'll have half a Guinness.' Mr Pat immediately shouts, 'Pint of Guinness for Mr Osman!'

Such were the times, or at least they were at Ipswich, and there are shades of Clough dragging his players down to the hotel bar late on the night before their 1979 League Cup Final and making it compulsory for each of them to contribute to the consumption of a dozen bottles of champagne. Garry Birtles suggested they were probably the only team in the country that got fined if they *didn't* go out on a Friday night.

Such stories may be amusing but they aren't apocryphal and there's a serious point lurking somewhere within. The creation of such an environment released the pressure that players at other clubs may have felt and built bonds within the squads that were vital to their unexpected successes. Mentioning this as a theory to John Wark elicited the response, 'I left Ipswich and went to Liverpool, and it was totally different – an immediate feeling of pressure – just a different environment. I know where you're coming from completely. I think it was a real factor.' The happy-go-lucky approach was a part of the recipe for success.

The removal of any feeling of pressure was relevant to Wark's manager as well as his team-mates. Robson would tell of the Cobbolds' insistence that nobody – neither they nor their guests – should talk about the match they had just seen once in the directors' lounge, stating that as they between them knew nothing about football they should restrict themselves to 'hello, well played, have a drink and what time's your bus home?' A certain Mr Clough would have been mightily impressed. Bryan Hamilton supports this, saying, 'Mr John took the pressure off with his aristocratic take on "win or lose, we're on the booze".'

But it's clear not only from Robson but from his players of the day that the brothers weren't simply valued as great hosts and entertainers – they were nobody's fools as astute and successful businessmen and were steadfast in their belief in their manager. Ultimately, that strength and wisdom played as much of a role in the future success as anything else at the club. For all Robson's building of a togetherness and true family club, it was the Cobbolds and their unique style and approach that initiated this spirit and created the environment in which it could flourish.

The sustained success was thus a consequence of this two-way respect and loyalty. Robson said, 'When results were going against me, in the early years, Mr John would tell the grumblers, "Our manager's name is not written on a chalkboard with a wet sponge nailed next to it,"' and he often referred to a wonderfully supportive and unpredictable environment, and to John and Patrick as lovable naughty schoolboys who never grew up and were every manager's dream. 'They never wavered in their support for me, even in the difficult first three seasons, when we finished 12th, 18th, and 19th and the crowd were chanting, "Robson out."' The Ipswich fans and public owe as great a debt to Mr John as they do to Bobby Robson himself. Allan Hunter was as succinct as ever – 'don't forget John Cobbold' – and Bob Harris acknowledges that it wouldn't in all probability happen this way today: 'Had it been the cut-throat world of modern football he would probably not have survived the two years of toil and struggle which allowed him the time to develop his team and ideas at Portman Road.'

The support wasn't limited to the boardroom. Elsie Robson, Anne McMenemy and Barbara Clough may seem unlikely names to have played a key part in this story, but the support of their families, particularly their wives, is seen by all three men as critical. It sustained them and was never taken for granted or forgotten. Indeed, McMenemy opens his autobiography with a dedication to his wife, Anne, whom he acknowledges as his greatest supporter 'without whom there would have been no story to tell'. And in this case there's no distinction between the three. Clough repeats the sentiment in his thanks to Barbara: 'Without Barbara's love, loyalty, understanding and remarkable tolerance, Brian Clough would not have succeeded or even survived.'

Despite their differences in personality, all three had strong marriages that lasted through many years. Jose Mourinho recalls Robson telling him how he felt Elsie saved his life. The players knew it too. Of Robson, Bryan Hamilton says, 'He had a lovely wife and family, and he was a very family-orientated man.' Whether this strength of relationship was a result of how they were brought up to appreciate the value of family is hard to say, but it was the second foundation of the platform of support they required.

The final pillar came from the football people they gathered around them. The most successful periods of Clough's career, whether at Hartlepool, Derby or Forest, came when he was working alongside his managerial partner (Clough never liked him to be referred to as his assistant), Peter Taylor. Even though there should be a virtual asterisk when Clough's feats are revisited, which gives due credit to his other half, this doesn't diminish the power of Clough's personality or his management skills, which were fundamental to his successes. The player who experienced more life with Clough than any other, John McGovern, gives credit to Taylor's contributions, but is in no doubt who was in charge and whose vision it was that was directing operations: 'One singer, one song – not four or five different people all talking to the players as you get today. That's why it worked.' Clough's striker Tony Woodcock, a callow and unremarkable player on Clough's arrival, and an established international by the time he left for top-level European football with Cologne four years later, concurs with McGovern: 'Peter was the talent scout and I saw Cloughie as the driving force. John McGovern would always say that separately they were good; together unbeatable.'

All the former Ipswich players I talked to were agreed on two things. Firstly, one of their manager's key strengths was surrounding himself with good people (and no shame in that; it doesn't detract from their own contribution to success as it's a key management skill in itself that they were astute enough to employ). For all the key player signings, building an effective team *off* the pitch was just as important and they all had their crucial lieutenants. Secondly, in having Ron Gray (according to Bryan Hamilton 'probably the biggest impact on Bobby because he found the players that made the difference – he was Bobby's eyes and ears in the game') and his respected team in place as his chief scout and regional scouts respectively, he was both a wise and fortunate man. Gray is talked of in glowing terms by his former charges – perhaps unsurprisingly given he set them on their career paths – but anybody who brings to the club the likes of George Burley, Trevor Whymark, Alan Brazil, Allan Hunter, Kevin Beattie, Russell Osman and John Wark has clearly played a blinder. It can also be no coincidence that for Ipswich and Southampton one of the strongest geographical areas of their scouting operations was the North East. While Robson rejected the recommendation of a young lad called Paul Gascoigne, Saints' scouting system did unearth another Geordie by the name of Alan Shearer.

For McMenemy the back-up support came from Jim Clunie, who came to join him as his assistant. He acknowledges the role Clunie's gruff, no-nonsense character and experience played in that crucial initial addressing of the ingrained indiscipline and establishing of his authority. Some of his former players may be relatively ambivalent about Clunie's abilities but McMenemy never was. And for all the initial awkwardness in their relationship, inevitable in the circumstances of McMenemy's arrival, he recalls how Ted Bates and he found a way to work together and acknowledges what a valued source of support and experience he was, not least during the FA Cup run of 1976. For all McMenemy's ultimate success it's right to recognise the impact of a man who spent 66 years at the club in various roles and whose initial efforts were the foundations on which McMenemy would now build. McMenemy was not fool enough to disregard or disrespect that level of experience.

Robson had his Cyril Lea and Ron Gray, McMenemy his Jim Clunie, and Clough had the likes of Jimmy Gordon, whom he always insisted contributed greatly to his managerial career. And, of course, he had, for a time, Peter Taylor. Support and loyalty, wheresoever it originated – directors, family or assistants – made the difference. And with it, things would gradually begin to turn around.

Turning the Tide

*'A successful man is one who can lay a
firm foundation with the bricks others
have thrown at him.'*

David Brinkley, US broadcaster

What are sometimes forgotten in the glut of trophies and memorable moments the clubs enjoyed are the relatively minor successes that came before them, although not by the managers nor by the players. Ipswich's winning of the FA Youth Cup in 1973 and again two years later was achieved by a group who would go on to form the basis of the heralded first teams from 75 to 81. Wark, Gates, Talbot, Osborne and Burley were all in those teams. That triumph added weight to everyone's belief that something was stirring at Portman Road. The players grew together and learned together. According to Russell Osman:

> The main strength in all those teams was that we knew each others' games. For example, in later years we knew Eric Gates was going to pull people all over the place in his unique role – or rather a role he played unlike, and better than, anyone else – and we knew what that meant for the rest of us. That began in the youth teams, and I think the Youth Cup was really significant because we started growing up together.

This sense of a telepathic understanding, echoed by Tony Woodcock when assessing the origins of Forest's success, was then honed to perfection on the training pitch, and then again at three o'clock on Saturday afternoons, but it found its source in these early experiences growing together as a group.

If this was the foundation at Ipswich, then Robson considered the 74/75 season the first demonstrable evidence of the great upswing and the first of his three successful teams. He knew this dramatic progress was the result of 'a fine scouting system, good judgement of players and plenty of quality time on the training ground. Naturally, dexterity in the transfer market was also required.' Robson reminded people that most of the star players of the next ten years came through the youth system, and recalled scouring Suffolk and Norfolk with a nit comb, doing a tremendous amount of scouting with Ron Gray. In time, the resultant flow of young local players into all three clubs was only to enhance further that bond between players, club and community. Mick Mills, Garry Birtles, Nick Holmes – these were all players rooted in the respective local areas who became cornerstones of their clubs' triumphs ahead.

The scouting was focused partly on finding these youngsters to join the club as apprentices at an early age, such as Wark and Burley, but of course the remit extended to unearthing the best 'diamonds' at a slightly older age as well. Ipswich, Southampton and Forest weren't the type of clubs that were going to be able to spend their way out of their state of stasis. The three managers realised success would require a three-pronged approach, which they all then followed over the decade. They would have to work with what they had; they would look to supplement with wise additions, often to provide experience and nous, at the realistic end of the transfer market; finally, they would have to develop young players, and therefore required not only a scouting operation of excellence, but a willingness to cover many miles personally on a cold

Tuesday night to see for themselves if they concurred with the recommendations. The youth policy became Robson's religion at Portman Road. He had no money – the quality of the club would have to be in the youth system and he dedicated himself to it with spectacular success.

Over the course of their eras of success, Robson leaned on his youth policy most heavily of the three. McMenemy was, in general, more inclined to go to the transfer market for bargains, and so too Clough. That said, McMenemy was proud of the pipeline he created via youth scouting and through the A team and reserves and he devoted much unseen time to it, building a development system worthy of a top-class club, which hadn't existed prior to his arrival. His former club secretary, Malcolm Price, once revealed in his match programme notes that after a home fixture against Chelsea, when everyone else had gone home, McMenemy was still there at 7.30pm giving an informative talk to a party of schoolboys, and wrote, 'If hard work and application behind the scenes are any criteria, this club can look forward to the day when all the endeavours bear the fruit they deserve.'

Indeed it could. Hard work and application were the minimum McMenemy demanded from his young players in return. All his teams contained at least one or two graduates. McMenemy accepted that since clubs like Southampton weren't going to be able to compete as transfer fees rose, it often had to be a case of grow your own. He considers his subsequent establishing of a new youth academy as one of his most important moves, and although he didn't often suggest as much, it was certainly one of his longest-lasting benefactions to the club. He developed that strong scouting network in his native North East, and a similar one in London, which was to produce an intake to the academy featuring the likes of Steve Williams, Reuben Agboola, the Wallace brothers, and many more who would go on to form part of the successful first teams.

From that point to the present day, Saints continued to burnish a reputation as a club that identified and developed talent as well as anyone – Alan Shearer, Matt Le Tissier, Theo Walcott, Gareth Bale and others offering compelling evidence. It began with McMenemy and his realisation that such development was going to be a necessary cornerstone of the team building to come. At the time, the likes of Pat Earles, Trevor Hebberd, Austin Hayes, Tony Sealy and fan favourite Tony Funnell would supplement his attack, although none made a place their own and were perhaps a sign that McMenemy was often one short of the ideal forward line he would have liked to reach the pinnacle. At the back, Malcolm Waldron and Manny Andruszewski would play valuable roles but those who bore greatest fruit from McMenemy's willingness to give young players their chance when he saw real talent were perhaps in midfield, where Williams and the underrated Graham Baker became fixtures. In his strongest teams of the early 80s, local boy Steve Moran and scouting prodigy Danny Wallace would have a significant impact. So, youth played its part but the manager's penchant for a big name remained.

Clough had a rather different way of going about it, given his preference for his sofa in Charnwood over Tuesday nights watching players at Crewe or Motherwell. In his case, the role Peter Taylor played in the spotting of both young talents and more seasoned pros who may have had more to offer than had previously been thought was of critical importance. But despite the difference in execution, all three understood the essential role young talent would have to play, even if Clough's reliance upon it came rather later, following Taylor's departure, when he rebuilt from 84 onwards.

It wasn't just the youth teams and their trophies that offered the first signs that the tide was turning. The first-team successes – Ipswich's Texaco Cup in 1973, Southampton's appearance in the final of the same competition the following year, and Forest's winning of the Anglo-Scottish Cup in late 1976 – may seem insignificant and quaint to some. These were, after all, rather oddball, manufactured competitions now seen as dripping with 70s football nostalgia by those committed enough to remember them. But the managers and their players are in no doubt at all that future glory would have been much less likely without them. For Tony Woodcock, who had been at the club since 1974 and not seen any obvious signs of impending success, the 'minor' trophy was a big step: 'We'd won a cup. That competition was where he first played me with Peter Withe and we hit it off.' From small acorns … the two forwards would combine to score 38 goals in winning two major trophies two years later. Of the team that would lift the European Cup a year after that, seven played a part in that final.

Bryan Hamilton had joined Ipswich at the time of the early struggles in 1971 and played a significant part in the transformation, and he's crystal clear about the evolution – where he felt it began and its contributory factors, the Texaco triumph being one of the most important among them.

Hamilton highlights four matches over two years that tell the story. On 7 September 1971 Ipswich played the Manchester United of Best and Charlton in the League Cup at Portman Road:

> We played United here and got a bit of a seeing-to, and the crowd were a bit 'unhappy' shall we say? And that's when I think Bobby was fortunate because John Cobbold could've done several things with him at that time, but he was not only an unbelievably nice man, but a very loyal man, and the route he went down was to totally support him. Then we went through that season and got a bit of stability without really lighting things up.

Ipswich fan Terry Hunt, writing in *Ipswich Town FC – The Glory Years Begin*, recalled the same game: 'United played us off the park. Uncharacteristically for the usually patient Ipswich fans the mood on the terraces turned ugly. There were widespread calls for Robson to be sacked.' He also endorses the view it was a turning point and that the support of John Cobbold was critical: 'Cobbold apologised to Robson for the fans' behaviour. A few days later he gave him the funds to buy Allan Hunter ... I am utterly convinced that if he hadn't been brave enough to stand by his man then the history of Ipswich Town Football Club would have been very different.'

Ipswich finished 13th that season, which was a distinct improvement on the previous two relegation campaigns but some way from where they would be 12 months later, which bears out Hamilton's recollection of a steadying of the ship that year. But it was the start of something, and he identifies the first match of the following season, coincidentally also against a star-studded United team, this time away from home, as the first true moment of realisation. (It's surely more than just coincidence that the match also heralded the debut of one Kevin Beattie, and the first-ever pairing of Beattie with his tutor Allan Hunter – a partnership critical to the turning of the tide.)

> We'd had a pre-season which was ordinary, we hadn't done well at all, but there were now a lot of good players – Allan Hunter vital, and Kevin just signed – and a lot of good youngsters coming through. First match of the season we went up to Old Trafford and we beat them 2-1. Trevor Whymark, who was an unbelievably good player who never got the acclaim he should have, got one, and I got one. From that moment we seemed to grow.

But it wasn't just such high-profile matches that made the team. By the end of that season Ipswich had finished fourth

– the first of nine top-six finishes in the next ten years before Robson's departure – but crucially in Hamilton's eyes they had also won the Texaco.

> Was the Texaco a big step? Yes, yes, more than anything – that was a *very* big step in the Robson era even if many saw it as a small step in terms of what we'd won. Not only did we beat some decent teams, but we beat Norwich in the final. There had been a winning habit after that United win, but after the Texaco there was a winning *mentality*.

It's an interesting distinction that connects all three teams of the period – the development of that mentality being a prerequisite for teams at smaller clubs who might aspire to challenge those with greater resources. And Hamilton is certain that, as with the evolutions at Forest and Southampton, the mentality was born out of the tightness of the unit. Match number four …

> It gave us togetherness. We went away, about 16 of us, to Barbados at the end of that season and we were so tight. Then we went pre-season to play Real Mallorca, which became anything but a friendly and we had a man sent off – unfairly – and we pulled together and there was no way we were going to let them beat us. I remember sitting in the dressing room and all the players who hadn't been in Barbados were back from international duty and so on, and all of a sudden, I had that feeling, that Bobby must've had several times, when I thought, *we can win with this group.* I thought, *We can play, and we can stick together and mix it if we need to as well.* I knew we could take on anybody and win anything – even if nobody else knew it yet, which was soon going to be one of our advantages – others didn't see what we

saw and didn't see it coming. Moments in time matter and the foundation was set from 1972 onwards. The Hunter signing, that Old Trafford performance, the Texaco win and Europe, the bringing-on of Beattie, Burley, Wark, and the coming together of that group that day in Spain were the key moments.

Moments matter indeed. Those matches that would become the 'sliding doors' weren't so far away. The tide had been turned and the most special of days were now just around the corner.

Glory Days 1975–1985

Glory Days 1975–1985

Pride, Community and Happy Bewilderment

'It was a decade of football the likes of which we will never see again.'

Sir Bobby Robson

I suppose we're all the emotional creation of the days that formed us, and 1975 to 1985 were the years that formed *me*. My personal attachment to them remains strong, beginning with my first autograph in the Milton Road car park shortly after Lawrie McMenemy's arrival in my home city of Southampton and culminating in my departure from school and the city in the very same summer that he also left for his native North East after the best part of 12 years. I have, therefore, a first-hand recollection of the sense of pride and community, not to mention blissfully happy bewilderment, our city felt as our unfathomable success grew.

As I gaze back across the vista of these years, forever drifting further away, I'm so grateful that I was able to participate personally in their delights. From a first visit to watch an unremarkable Second Division match on a dark November afternoon to a nonsensical FA Cup win seven months later; from watching Hull and Hereford one minute to welcoming Marseille and Anderlecht the next; from Pat Earles and Paul Gilchrist to Kevin Keegan, Charlie George and Frank Worthington – it still has the quixotic nature of a dream. This is, I assume, why 45 years on I still get an ache in the pit of my stomach and a thumping heart every time the results come through. Given my lack of any real attachment to the place these days, in a way it's a strange allegiance but it's an allegiance, nonetheless, formed by that sense of belonging to something that can't be erased. This is Lawrie's lasting legacy to me personally. It's something all committed football supporters will recognise. Ipswich follower Tim Smith understands my turmoil. For him Ipswich is still home, a home to which he travels every other Saturday if he can, to the same ground with which he grew up and he has no doubt that the Robson years were what cemented that everlasting bond.

While they were years of unparalleled success for each of these clubs, these ten years specifically were also significant for English football in a wider context as the last time a group of smaller clubs from outside the perceived big-city elite upset the accepted order with a period of sustained success and abstruse achievement. They stimulate memories in fans of all clubs of a time when clubs, players and managers were connected to their peoples in a manner not possible today. For those of us whose adolescence bridged these years, they're tremendously evocative – whether in relation to football or life in general. Personally, I can still close my eyes and walk through a late 1970s Saturday and its unalterable rhythm: *Multi-Coloured Swap Shop*, *Football Focus*; Mum's homemade meatloaf and marmite gravy (better than it sounds); to and from The Dell down Hill Lane; half-time Bovril watching the men in white coats hanging half-time score slates on to hooks along the advertising hoardings; the rush back to the car in time for *Sports Report*; and home for a kip before parental resurrection in time for *Match of the Day*. I told you I was a nostalgist. The reason *Too Good to Be Forgotten* has prioritised this particular timespan is to remind those who were there how special the period was and to explain to those who weren't how such a thing could come about.

The country, too, was a very different place in 1985 to ten years previously, changed beyond recognition over the previous decade. And 1975 was a fascinating time in the political and social history of the country – a time of apparent stasis in which things *were* actually happening imperceptibly, as with our three football clubs, that were to have an impact we couldn't anticipate at that moment, including the arrival of a certain Margaret Thatcher as the new leader of Her Majesty's opposition.

That this should happen within a month of another leader of strong convictions and distinctive personality arriving at Nottingham Forest Football Club isn't the only strange parallel of timing and evolution between the political and social developments of the time and the stories of our subjects. Given the mining communities from which they came, and their support of those people whose dangerous work kept them afloat, it feels uncanny that Clough's arrival at Forest in 1975 should come less than a year after the settling of one successful miners' strike, and McMenemy's departure in the summer of 85 should be confirmed just three months after a second, unsuccessful one that shifted the political balance and changed the nature of the country and its industry forever. The nation had moved from the three-day week to the brink of the 'Big Bang' in the City of London and from industries that were the preserve and salvation of the working people so dear to the three men to a financial services-driven society populated and controlled by a very different social demographic.

In 1974, in the aftermath of that first strike, the embattled Conservative Prime Minister, Edward Heath, called a General Election, posing the potentially dangerous question, 'Who governs?' The public of the time gave him his answer. In the short term it was one that ushered in a Labour Government. But in terms of who governed, by 1985 nobody was in any doubt, for better or for worse, that Margaret Thatcher did. Given their respective political sympathies there's some irony that the determination of Clough, McMenemy and Robson to establish total autonomy and impose discipline and tough medicine where necessary should so closely mirror Thatcher's own philosophy. Clough in particular, one suspects, would have been apoplectic at the comparison but that can't disguise the similarities in approach and, in some facets, character, and it wouldn't be utter fantasy to suspect he might recognise a similar strength of character and harbour a grudging respect. In building their success the three were going to have to channel something of the Iron Lady, and 'who governs?' was to be a question they would each have to pose as their tenancies at the three clubs began. None of them would be for turning.

From the season of Southampton's unforgettable triumph at Wembley, the glory days ran to that which ended not just with McMenemy's departure but with the departure of English clubs from European competition for the next five seasons in the wake of the events at the Heysel Stadium European Cup Final (possibly, and sadly, the inevitable conclusion to the fan violence in Europe that began in earnest with Leeds United fans and their own European Cup Final ten years before … in 1975). Given Europe had played such a part in the glory days for these clubs and managers, the air went very rapidly out the balloon in that instant.

What emerges in the following recollection is a story of special talent and character. These weren't simply extremely able football men but true personalities whose profile at times transcended the game itself in an era when some might agree with the words of Rodney Marsh that football in England was 'a grey game, played by grey men, on grey days'. I happen to *disagree*. There may have been no live matches to fill a late Sunday afternoon (or Saturday lunchtime or Monday evening, and so on ad infinitum). The grounds may have been down-at-heel and the pitches often of a nature that would cause the postponement of a Sunday league game today. (Steve Williams seemed to have these in mind when asking how good the likes of Channon and Best would have been on today's consistently pristine surfaces. 'They were unplayable in the mud … blimey, what would they have been like today?') The greatest global stars may not have been regularly paraded in the First Division. But these were precious days in the lives of many a baby-boomer football fan.

Obsession

'To have any long-term success as a coach or in any position of leadership, you have to be obsessed in some way.'

Pat Riley, Chief Executive, Miami Heat basketball

The next ten years were to take their careers, their provincial clubs and their communities to places they had never been before. Ten years. Not a one-off moment of glory. How on earth did they do it?

Pat Riley's words above give us a good part of the answer. They had a complete obsession with the game. McMenemy chose to title his autobiography *A Lifetime's Obsession*. Robson's every living moment was consumed by his passion for the game and his drive to improve himself and his players. His wife Elsie claimed that they had an agreement that when he was at home it would be a haven in which they didn't talk football, which may well be true but there's a strong suspicion that Bobby's mind was on the game even if his mouth wasn't giving him away. Alex Ferguson said that whenever he saw his friend, he thought of the word *enthusiastic*. 'There are no grey areas – you get that passion from him whenever you meet him. He was everything that was good about the game. He loved the game … and the game loved him.' And the player who probably had more affection for Robson than any other, Paul Gascoigne, found in his England manager a kindred spirit in that 'he was totally obsessed with football'.

Brian Clough may not have displayed the same commitment to the Robson and McMenemy dictum of 'first in, last to leave' every day, but his own obsession was most obvious in his staying too long – he could, and surely should, have taken his leave on a high somewhere before the completion of his 18 years, but he couldn't let go.

Obsession begets enthusiasm, and this too was a common trait as Ferguson suggested, with Gary Lineker considering Robson the most enthusiastic person he ever met in football, with an unimpeachable love for the game and a capacity to see the best in everyone. Positivity and empathy are oft-repeated words when talking to people about their affection and admiration for Robson. Mel Henderson at Ipswich noted that Robson answered every single letter he received personally 'and I bet you don't see that these days. Bobby was a unique man.'

George Caulkin of The Athletic online football platform produced a fascinating podcast based on a personal interview with Robson late in his life. On TalkSPORT, presenter Andy Jacobs asked Caulkin a semi-rhetorical question: 'Did any manager ever love football more than Bobby Robson?' Caulkin responded, 'That was just it. It was this lifetime's obsession with football. He had this incredible zest for life as well as football which was part of his management and drove everything.' Jacobs's co-presenter Paul Hawksbee shared his own memory that 'there was always this incredible enthusiasm whenever he talked of anything football related, and that used to shine through', recounting a story from when he was editing *Goal* magazine and the staff went to play a six-a-side tournament abroad at which Robson was persuaded to coach them as part of the PR plan. Apparently he threw himself at the task as if these boys on a jolly were playing in the Champions League.

This energy and enthusiasm not only ran through the three men themselves, but they shared an ability to transfer it to those in their charge. Alex Ferguson had Robson in mind but could just as well have been referring to Clough or

McMenemy when he said, 'People talk about what makes a great manager. It's someone who can create an energy source … and you can't go to the chemist and buy that.'

The last words on obsession, from the documentary *More Than a Manager*, go to Bobby Robson himself: 'Do I need the hassle of what football does to you? Yes. Because I love it. As long as I feel this way I want to keep working. I'm immersed in football. It's my god.' Those whose happiness was linked to the fortunes of the clubs they managed were never going to be short-changed.

Magic Moments

'It's the best football this town has seen in its life.'

Bobby Robson

At the start I insisted that this story isn't primarily about the trophies. Or if it is, then it's about the knock-on effect they still have today rather than the statistical detail that has been covered elsewhere many times before. But in the space of 24 months, Southampton, then Forest and Ipswich, turned the football world upside down.

On a hot, sunny May Day in 1976 – the sort of day that for a while seemed to be as much a part of the FA Cup Final as the presentation of the trophy – Saints beat odds so long they were disappearing over the horizon to beat Manchester United and win their first-ever major trophy. In the process a city came out for a shared celebration the like of which hadn't been seen before and hasn't been since. Two years later Ipswich repeated the trick – maybe not outsiders to the extent of Saints before them but still unfancied by most to beat the London powerhouse that was Arsenal. The same sweltering heat, a similarly popular and unheralded match-winning goalscorer, a 1-0 win, and a reception in the hometown of a similar magnitude.

Two Saturdays previously, Forest's 'they'll not win it – they'll fall away soon' season (the prediction failing to take into account the past deeds of Brian Clough) had culminated in winning the league title with that Peter Shilton-inspired goalless draw at Coventry. Thus, Clough had taken a second unfashionable East Midlands club to such heights, and even greater glory awaited. Having already secured the League Cup exactly a month earlier, that made four major honours for the three clubs in two momentous years. Each one of them led to parties laced with incredulity in numbers almost ten times greater than their ground capacities, reminiscent of VE Day celebrations – publics coming together as one in a common moment of pride and elation.

But these successes alone don't define the glory days, particularly from a supporter's perspective. Over five years these three clubs landed two FA Cups, two League Cups, a league title and European and UEFA Cup wins, but the memories that linger aren't confined to these. They are also of *moments* – special occasions that people would never have imagined they might experience. In *The Fans Behind the Legend*, Forest supporter Simon Robinson talks of the magic of suddenly, in 1977, travelling away to all those First Division grounds he had only ever seen on *Star Soccer* and *Match of the Day*. These pleasures, taken for granted by the established elite clubs, were to be treasured by the provincial fans. And as special experiences go, for many, European nights were the ultimate.

The opening of the door to the unique magic of European football was an exciting consequence of these victories. For Ipswich this was something of an extension of the special nights they had enjoyed in the previous five years. Although Southampton had had one previous attempt – a first-round exit in 1971 in the UEFA Cup – and Forest two Fairs Cup seasons in the 60s but a sum total of only three ties, for these clubs it felt like a genuinely new adventure.

Significant success in Europe was something that evaded McMenemy, while Clough and Robson brought home silverware. But my personal experience of the 1976/77 European Cup Winners' Cup run is that it was an exotic fairy tale, even if I didn't have my father's wider perspective and understanding that this was a truly remarkable turn of events for such a club and city. The fact that we didn't win the thing in May will never dilute the memories of Southampton 4 Olympique Marseille 0, or Southampton 2 Anderlecht 1 on nights of febrile excitement.

The Ipswich teams prior to the 1981 UEFA Cup success didn't bring home any European trophies, but they were the ones who prepared the ground by starting that special relationship with European football. (Their previous fleeting acquaintance with the European Cup in 1962 having ended at the first round proper.) Only 13 months on from that Old Trafford victory, which Bryan Hamilton cites as the beginning of the beginning, Ipswich were beating Real Madrid at Portman Road. A year later the locals were watching Ipswich 4 Lazio 0.

Hamilton remembers:

> Europe was special. The supporters will tell you that – the lights on, the atmosphere, the European 'smell' was there. We were never beaten in Europe at Portman Road. It was important because there's not a big rugby or cricket presence and there's only one team in Suffolk. People talk to me to this day about those early European nights and I'm glad they still do.

Having myself experienced those Marseille and Anderlecht nights at The Dell, this spoke to me. Smell can be a most evocative sense, and the idea of the aroma of a European night rings true. That such continental giants could be beaten at the homes of these clubs may in some part be attributable to the grounds themselves. Nobody wanted to come and play at the City Ground, The Dell or Portman Road when they were bursting at the seams. As difficult an assignment as it might have been, they would probably have preferred to be at Anfield. I remember the incongruity of watching the likes of

Jeff Wealands and Jeff Hemmerman as we hosted Hull City in February and, the following month, Anderlecht's Robbie Rensenbrink and Arie Haan, both soon to be playing in a World Cup Final – something akin to the idea of Red Rum or Frankel racing on Southampton Common. (For the record, we beat Anderlecht and drew with Hull, which was Saints all over at the time.) The managers might have bemoaned the somnolence of their crowds on occasions but on nights like these there were few more intimidating places to play. For Ipswich never to be beaten at home in Europe throughout this period is an astonishing achievement and there can be little doubt that Portman Road itself and the people inside it played a significant role.

Looking at the season-by-season achievements listed in the pages to come still creates a sense of wonder. In considering the 'how' we should follow the managers' lead and keep it simple. The recipe for the glory days was no more complex than the application of the various skills that populate the chapters ahead. Easy to commit to paper – less easy to do.

Of course, it remains a nagging source of disappointment for Saints and Ipswich fans that they never quite made it to winning the league, or that a possible double for Southampton in 1984, and at one stage a distinctly likely treble for Ipswich in 1981, never came to pass. These would have undoubtedly been the tangible evidence of the clubs' competitiveness forevermore. Churlish though it might be to point out, in Southampton's case Steve Williams's belief that they were always one jigsaw piece away from being the finished article for winning the title is more plausible than his suggestion that three points for a win would have got them there. In fact, in 1981 that would have seen them move just one place ahead of their sixth-placed finish. And 1982 also gave the lie to the theory – three points for a win arrived that season and first place did not.

The truth is that across these ten years Robson and McMenemy won only three major trophies between them, although they were so close to adding more that they could be touched. But for the fans it was also about the quality of the football they were now watching every week, and the entertainment – you went to the ground fuelled with the anticipation of another day of excitement. Entertainment was considered by all three managers as a fundamental part of what the game should offer its supporters and in the end their ability to deliver it was just as important as silverware in the cupboard.

Mick Channon says the huge enjoyment he got from his three 'blinding years' after he returned to The Dell in 1979 was down to the attacking football Saints were playing, which was making them the second-favourite team of a large number of football fans. It was a team of attractive method rather than ruthless efficiency. After a couple of seasons Channon was joined by the underrated but hugely influential David Armstrong – another smart piece of jigsaw assimilation by McMenemy – who said the same thing: 'The way we played the game was a pleasure to be part of. I felt that as a player so I can only imagine what our fans felt about it.' A terrible shame that such a humble and respected man isn't still around for me to be able to give him my answer. The way McMenemy wanted to play was also part of the sales prospectus for the bigger stars. Kevin Keegan said of his decision to sign, 'The other attraction for me was Lawrie McMenemy. I could tell straight away that I was going to enjoy playing for him. On his watch Saints were not short of what he called "violinists".'

That nagging feeling, fun though it was, of a sense of missed opportunity lingers with players, fans and manager at Ipswich too – specifically those involved in 1981. They can, however, approach the memory of falling short slightly differently, taking consolation from Europe in a way McMenemy never could. Robson did see the loss of a treble, which at one stage that season was more probable than possible, as his greatest regret but also insisted that, for him, winning a European trophy was an even greater endorsement of what the club achieved and he valued it more than their FA Cup victory, although he knew many players and directors took the opposite view. John Wark is one of that number for a particular reason: 'I still make the FA Cup the best thing I ever achieved, because it was the *first thing*.' This element of achieving something for the first time ever was another reason the glory days are cherished – perhaps it wasn't the *number* of trophies that made the difference but rather their historical significance and their rarity.

The players of 81 agree with their manager that the frustration was greater because it was not through any lack of ability or mental strength that they landed only one of three trophies that year. Robson identified a lack of squad strength, of numbers, which explained the narrow failure to win the league in those years. When injuries struck, his only option was to call on youth. He would shuffle and reshuffle but come up short. He felt he had perhaps 14 championship-winning-calibre players when he needed 19.

John Wark still knows the stats, and the fact he can reference them in an instant off the top of his head suggests it still hurts: 'We played 66 games that season. Villa [who won the title] played 46.' For a squad of 14 those extra 1,800 minutes were surely the decisive factor.

In conversation it was clear it still gnaws away at Russell Osman too: 'Injuries cost us. Kevin Beattie broke his arm in the cup semi. We lost George Burley at Easter.' And it wasn't just injuries but other things various that seemed to conspire. 'Oh, the way we lost that FA Cup semi-final … of course we lost Kevin, but even before that he missed with a header from six yards, which he never did. He did everything right and headed it down, but the pitch was so rock-hard it bounced off the ground and over the bar from inside six yards!'

Bill Shankly insisted that when he packed up he didn't want to be remembered for victories and trophies, but for playing the game the right way. Ultimately, in referring to the glory days, we should be talking not just about the trophies, but about the excitement, the glorious moments and the opportunities to dream as never before that were afforded us over the next ten unforgettable seasons.

1975/76

Southampton
6th Second Division
FA CUP WINNERS

Nottingham Forest
8th Second Division
Clough's first full season

Ipswich Town
6th First Division
UEFA Cup round 2

And the ball is played through to Bobby Stokes, and Bobby Stokes shoots and Bobby Stokes scores! Oh, what a turn-up this could be. It's Manchester United nil, Southampton one!'

The incredulous words of radio commentator Peter Jones remain fixed in my head today … 82 minutes in, Turner to Channon, to McCalliog, to Stokes … and on to history.

The 1975/76 season was unremarkable for Forest, a consolidation of the previous season's major step forward for Ipswich, utterly unforgettable for Southampton, and the making of Lawrie McMenemy.

Any optimism regarding the first full season under Clough at Forest was punctured by their first ten league matches, which produced just two wins and a place in the relegation zone. An improvement of sorts thereafter saw them finish in eighth place, which was respectable unless you considered Clough's arrival to be a guarantee of promotion. Perhaps the most significant moments of their season would be the signings of full-backs Frank Clark from Newcastle and Colin Barrett from Manchester City. Unheralded at the time, the first careful additions were being made. Both would go on to win European Cup medals within four years.

The season before had confirmed the progress being made by Ipswich under Robson, following fourth place in the previous two seasons, with third in the table and a run to an FA Cup semi-final and narrow replay defeat to West Ham. In those terms, 75/76 could be termed a regression, with a sixth-placed finish and early cup exits. They were, however, in Europe again, and despite a second-round defeat by eventual finalists Club Brugge, that was a fair indication that the longer-term trend remained upwards. Liverpool took another title, while Ipswich were never really in the race, the story of the season being the Queens Park Rangers team of Gerry Francis and Stan Bowles that almost snatched a league title nobody could have foreseen. It was the season's end that saw a signing just as significant as those at Forest, with Paul Mariner arriving to replace David Johnson. Some questioned the wisdom at the time, but it proved to be another shrewd evolution of the team by Robson. Within two years Mariner would have his hands on an FA Cup winners' medal.

Southampton's second attempt to get back to the First Division never really threatened its objective, with sixth place underwhelming for a squad dotted with past and present internationals. The suave confidence of the Channons, Osgoods and McCalliogs seemed incongruous in an environment that took them to the likes of Orient and Oldham. The Achilles heel of poor away form, which over the years was never to be completely cured and would ultimately cost them a title, was in startling evidence with their first nine away matches delivering two draws and seven defeats. Despite being nigh-on unbeatable at home, losing 13 times away was never going to be compatible with ambitions of promotion.

Cups, however, were to prove more to the liking of McMenemy's strings section, in particular. What happened in the league was to be forgotten forever in the *annus mirabilis* that would culminate in the most remarkable FA Cup triumph. McMenemy duly became the first of the trio to land a major prize at these clubs and the one that, at the time, was still considered the most coveted and famous in domestic club football anywhere in the world. The ego that had always been a part of the proud guardsman and been only slightly damaged by the previous two seasons now received the plaudits to sustain it, although not in an unpleasant manner, through the rest of his time at the club. And why not? He deserved it. Personal experience allows me to confirm that there was an electricity and positivity in the city, and a sudden comradeship within its community, not matched before or since, as the whole of Southampton and its considerable catchment area enjoyed its moment in the sun.

From that sliding doors Hughie Fisher goal in round three, as the draws consecutively paired Saints with Blackpool, West Brom and Bradford City, the sense that something was afoot grew across the city – a feeling that was significantly enhanced when the draw for the semi-final set them against Third Division Crystal Palace rather than the might of Manchester United or Derby County. The seemingly everlasting month of happy fever between the successful semi-final and the club's first-ever trip to Wembley had the feeling of a 28-day jubilee-style communal party a year ahead of its time as a whole area became consumed with Southampton's football. The only sobering element was the widely held belief that, against the resurgent Manchester United of Tommy Docherty, recently placed third in the First Division, Saints had next to no chance as a team junior by a league to their opponents.

In the cup final edition of *Shoot!* magazine, 20 players were asked for their predictions. Once they had given their opinions the result came down 18-2 in favour of United (Peter Lorimer and Peter Houseman being the only two who would have beaten the bookies, for those who might be interested). But not everyone felt that way, least of all Lawrie McMenemy and the majority of his players. In United they saw a talented group of young players with virtually no experience of the big occasion. Looking round their own dressing room they saw established internationals, former cup finalists and winners, and some hard-bitten pros who had been waiting for this day for years without much expectation of it eventually arriving. All possessed temperaments more suited than that of their opponents to rising to the challenge of such an occasion. Violinists and road sweepers.

The Southampton mix was the far better one for the occasion and it proved decisive in producing the greatest day in the club's history. Peter Osgood credits McMenemy with the perfect management of half-time in the final: 'Lawrie was his usual calming influence. He was really accurate in telling us how it would go and instilled confidence in us. He was superb.' If Osgood had any concerns that he had signed on the back of what seemed far-fetched promises from the manager when he told him he was going to help him win major trophies, he wasn't concerned now: 'At five o'clock on that scorching hot day in May 1976 no one doubted Lawrie McMenemy anymore.' He had indeed announced himself. To quote Robert Browning: 'A minute's success pays the failure of years.'

This team balance that won them the cup hadn't happened by chance. It came from McMenemy's foresight in understanding the benefits of assembling a team that had a real blend of characters, complementary abilities and youth supplementing experience. He then demonstrated the ability to create a team. It was a vision and a skill also possessed by

Robson and Clough and was the starting point for everything they were all now to achieve – they were piecing together their jigsaws.

The Jigsaw

'Putting old heads together with young legs was
what I did at Southampton. I think that mixture
helped in the dressing room and brought success.'

Lawrie McMenemy

I could've gone to Arsenal, my home club, at the age
of 22 but I didn't because I could see that Lawrie was
building a team – one which was already better than
Arsenal's. Then, when I did go four years later and
Arsenal were struggling, it was clear why. Arsenal then
were a collection of stars but not a team – they didn't
fit together. At Saints we were a real team. There's
a huge difference when you're trying to win football
matches. Players wanted to play for the likes of Clough
and McMenemy because they could see the sort of
teams they were building.

So says Steve Williams, whose years at The Dell all but
mirrored McMenemy's, joining as an apprentice in 1975 and
departing for Highbury in the summer of 84.

Each man believed future success would be based on
assembling this jigsaw – building a team and a squad with
the ideal fit, which placed the right pieces in the right place
and contained a mix of talents, all of which had a role to
play, and players who understood and accepted those roles
with complete clarity. They would never have claimed to
be erudite intellectuals, but they possessed a felicity in their

communication hugely effective in instructing and coercing a room full of footballers.

McMenemy would refer to how he assembled such teams as a proper balance of old heads and young legs, each to a high degree dependent on the other. He saw this as the greatest fascination of management. Peter Rodrigues says of McMenemy, 'It was a matter of square pegs in square holes. He knew what each player could do and wouldn't necessarily improve them individually – it was more fitting the pieces together and he was brilliant at that.' Rodrigues sees this creation of interdependence and the complete trust in your team-mates it required as the most common thread between the teams the three managers built.

McMenemy's approach was replicated by Robson at Ipswich, if not so much in his 75 and 78 teams, then certainly in the supreme 81 version. The lead violinists in this case were the Dutch pair Arnold Mühren and Frans Thijssen. Robson said of that team, 'We had a mixture of continental talent and some really high-quality homegrown players. It was very fluent, very cohesive and every player gelled. The system ran like clockwork.' Robson's philosophy was based on his goal of entertainment. In his first press conference as manager at Barcelona many years later he simply said, 'Football is about entertainment and what we hope to bring is good football – and we need players who can change the game.' Tim Smith, as a fan watching on, also monitored the piecing together of the jigsaw: 'Bobby had the talent, but he also brought in some hard-nosed professionals and built a team which had a mix. Some of them weren't Suffolk boys – although funnily enough, they are now.'

If simplicity was the watchword when it came to playing philosophy, the more apposite one in completing a jigsaw that would deliver success was *clarity*. Players gelling was the key, and according to both John Wark and John McGovern it was a simple matter of knowing their roles and not being asked to do something they couldn't. 'Everyone knew what they were doing – everyone knew their jobs,' says Wark. Robson felt the 81 team worked so well because he found a system to suit every single player in the team. McGovern credits the success of the team building at Forest to the same clarity, and David Armstrong saw the philosophy in McMenemy too, saying that he kept it simple and just wanted to make sure everyone playing was confident in what they had to do.

At Forest, as at his previous clubs, Clough would be irritated by the supporters and the media belittling John McGovern and his role in his teams. Here was a player Clough took with him wherever he went and chose as his captain at Forest, and he was adamant they wouldn't have been picking up any European Cups without him. McGovern was the personification of Clough's simple game creed. Like his manager he was also a very effective leader of men.

For each club, and each jigsaw laid out, there were certain individuals who would be central to the effective completion of that puzzle. For all McGovern's importance to the team, the two players brought in as the cement that would bind together the bricks of the existing players Clough had reinvented were Peter Shilton and Kenny Burns. Shilton – the only player to play for all three men at some point – was generally recognised as being worth at least ten fewer goals conceded and ten points gained on his own, and the outstanding choice if the objective was to become harder to beat. Clough always felt that Shilton was the difference – that he changed the dynamic of the team.

That was something not lost on McMenemy either, who in 1982, probably accepting that a vulnerable and inconsistent defence had done for his chances of the title in the previous two seasons, took Shilton off his mate's hands. 'Too late,' they cried; Kevin Keegan had pushed McMenemy to make precisely this signing six months earlier when Saints hit the top of the league. The fact it didn't happen at that time certainly contributed to Keegan's frustration at what he saw as a lack of ambition and ruthlessness in pursuit of the ultimate prize, which led to his departure that summer and the enduring regret of the Saints fans (and manager) that the two would never play together for the club. As the final piece of McMenemy's jigsaw was put in place, a vital existing piece went missing. Shilton duly did help turn Southampton's into one of the best defences in the country, something on which they built their assault on a double in 1984. It was the same year Keegan retired at Newcastle. We Saints fans can never shake the feeling that, had he stayed, that double would have been ours and McMenemy would have achieved all he had set out to. The perfect jigsaw for McMenemy was therefore not quite completed and, in that moment, it was destined never to be so, but he only missed out by one piece, as Steve Williams suggested.

There are few connected with Ipswich who don't reference the signings of first Allan Hunter as an established pro, and then Kevin Beattie as an apprentice, and the subsequent relationship between the two as critical in the club's emergence. Beattie is remembered with fondness and a tinge of regret that a talent that Robson believed was as close to Duncan Edwards as he would ever see was compromised by significant injuries, which ultimately curtailed what could and should have been a career as one of the all-time British greats. Some feel he's in that category regardless. However, Beattie was a youngster with a difficult home background and needed handling with care if he was to make good on his ability and play his key role in the club's success. This was, after all, a home-loving and unassuming player who rather than join the England camp on his first international call-up decided to return home to Carlisle and play dominoes with his dad in his local pub until tracked down and persuaded to change his mind.

Although Robson undoubtedly had the empathy to handle Beattie well, both were fortunate that the other pieces of the jigsaw, both on the pitch and off it, worked to Beattie's advantage. Bryan Hamilton explained his take on this:

Sliding doors. Hughie Fisher's last-minute equaliser keeps Saints in the 1976 FA Cup. 119 days later they had won the trophy. Moments matter

Three of a kind? The similarities of the three men stretched to their love of Sinatra. They would all take on board the words of 'My Way'

In the blood. The seething passion for football in the North East of England and their connection to that place never left them

Robson's life view and values were heavily influenced by the sobering experience of the Langley Park mine in Durham at 15 years old

Both Clough and McMenemy credited Alan Brown as the mentor who did more than anyone to shape their footballing lives and methods

Robson leaves his office following the sack at Fulham. Both he and McMenemy were hit hard and toughened up by the experience of losing jobs early on

McMenemy's expression suggests a wariness of Terry Paine's involvement in the announcement of his first star signing. Both Robson and McMenemy had to wrest control from antagonistic senior players on their arrivals

Brian Clough's arrival at Forest in January 1975 preceded Margaret Thatcher's as leader of the Conservatives by just 36 days. The two shared many traits even though Clough may have been apoplectic at the comparison

The power of personality. Both McMenemy and Clough cultivated strong media profiles to enhance their personal impact, though the latter was the more instantly recognisable outside the game

John Cobbold, the inimitable Ipswich chairman welcomes Robson. The old Etonian was to back his manager through thick and thin. Loyal directors, supportive wives, and able lieutenants were pillars critical to success

Turning the tide. Robson poses with his trusted lieutenants Charlie Woods, Cyril Lea and Bobby Ferguson before the 73/74 season. Directly in front of Robson sits the Texaco Cup – the 'minor' trophy that Bryan Hamilton believes was crucial to the success to come.

A youthful Tony Woodcock in the first leg of the 1976 Anglo Scottish Cup Final. Like Hamilton at Ipswich, Woodcock, his team-mates and his manager never underestimated the importance of this first success

It wasn't just the trophies … the European nights in febrile atmospheres were special. Here David Peach puts Southampton ahead in a Cup Winners' Cup quarter-final with crack side Anderlecht in 1977. The tie was narrowly lost but the memories are not

Peter Shilton and Kenny Burns celebrate the title in April 1978. Building the jigsaw was a shared skill. Clough always believed these two were the pieces that completed his picture

'How on earth did he manage that lot?' asked Peter Rodrigues, remembering McMenemy's skill at handling his beloved 'rascals'

A simple game. A shared belief that football was no more complicated than 'pass to someone with the same coloured shirt on' proved highly effective. In Robson's case it was Ferenc Puskas's Hungarians who shaped that philosophy

Allan would say Kevin is one of the best players he's ever played with – an unbelievable athlete – but Kevin was also lucky because he had a manager who totally supported him, and then on the pitch, on one side he had Mick Mills – outstanding player and outstanding leader – and on the other he had Allan Hunter. He was allowed to make mistakes and these people supported him and guided him, and that's why he became probably the best player Ipswich ever developed.

Hamilton suggested that Beattie needed not just love but 'tough love' and that Hunter played a key role as a mentor off the pitch as well as on. Beattie and Hunter together were a vital cog – and Hunter himself should not be underplayed in this. Hamilton refers to him as 'arguably the most influential player Bobby signed for Ipswich, because he allowed others to grow around him'. Spending time with Allan Hunter you get a sense of a combination of strength and generosity. It's easy to imagine the empathy and the support given to a young man like Beattie – protection and the arm around the shoulder as well as a footballing education – and the role he played in fitting him into Robson's plan. It was all about combinations that worked; about the *fit*. This was what putting the jigsaw together meant – more than just good players and good *young* players but the right mix, and a support system that allowed them to blossom.

Ipswich's 1978 FA Cup win came via what Robson considered the second significant team he built, and again he referenced the balance in that team. It was built on hardworking players. Talbot and Osborne were the engine and John Wark could score goals. And the manager would later call his 1981 creation 'the perfect jigsaw'.

Clough always believed in balance as well as talent. In reflecting on his 1979 European Cup winners, he said, 'We had the perfect balance across the middle of the pitch ...

we varied it, including others at times, but always bearing in mind that same sense of balance.' The personnel might occasionally have to change but the structure remained the same. He possibly erred more on the side of solid characters and 'legs' than flair in comparison with McMenemy, although the latter also believed that good football came from the balance between his violinists and road sweepers. True, he often seemed to have rather a large orchestra and not too many on the dust, although this was perception to an extent and McMenemy was always striving to get that balance just right.

But where there was doubt, McMenemy tended towards the star players for what they could do and for whom he had such an affection. That he was always thinking long term and believed such players would be needed when the challenges became greater is apparent in his notes in the match programme for the last home match of 1974/75, the first back in the Second Division. Summing up his thoughts on why he hadn't succeeded in delivering the fans' expected first-attempt promotion, he suggested his team had taken a long while to get used to the direct, organised style in the lower league. But he implied he was taking the longer-term view and wouldn't compromise on the use of his flair players, whom he would need in time. He cited Bristol City as one of the best organised teams in the division with a lack of any one star player, but he offered the personal opinion that they would struggle if they did get promoted in a way Saints wouldn't, as a result of the composition of the team.

If that might have seemed a little impertinent to some for a manager who had achieved a relegation and no promotion in his first 18 months, it does evidence the scale of his ambition. From the start he wasn't planning purely for a return to the top division – he was planning to take it by storm. (His perspicacity was also borne out. City were promoted the following year and were relegated again after four seasons of struggle.)

By the time he built his most exciting team in the early 80s, the foundations were midfielders Steve Williams, David Armstrong and Graham Baker but even they could hardly have been termed blue collar – if they did do some road sweeping, they must have been taking music lessons on the side. But it was this fondness for the violinists and the attacking if slightly erratic football they produced that seduced the big names to come to Southampton in the first place. It was on signing Kevin Keegan that McMenemy had not only produced his most jaw-dropping piece of transfer derring-do but had acquired the ultimate hybrid player – the virtuoso council worker, if you like: the road-sweeping violinist.

As for young players supporting older heads as he built his teams, Steve Moran was a young striker McMenemy had spotted personally playing schoolboy football and he became a key player in what was probably his most exciting team, up front alongside Keegan and Channon or Charlie George. Moran knew McMenemy saw the benefit of adding the young legs to a forward line of older heads. It worked well enough that for a time Moran almost outshone Keegan and he became the Professional Footballers' Association (PFA) Young Player of the Year.

Another example of blending energy with know-how involved Alan Ball. The World Cup winner – in the experienced, or perhaps even veteran category by then – conducted the Saints' midfield from 1976/77 to 1978/79, taking them to promotion and a League Cup Final. He returned as part of the stellar 81 and 82 teams, by this time in his late 30s. He was exactly what McMenemy was looking for in the evolution of the team – a senior player who instantly earned respect and in McMenemy's view took the team to a new level – initially to target promotion and then to marshal them against more challenging First Division opposition. McMenemy would tell the likes of Steve Williams and Nick Holmes that they were to be Ball's legs – that he couldn't do much of his own running but, if they did it for him, he could not only win a match for them but also teach them something into the bargain. It was similar with Peter Osgood, of whose arrival Hughie Fisher says, 'Fantastic guy, great personality, great in the dressing room. Tremendous ability, and he taught me a few things when he came.' One assumes Hughie wasn't referring solely to learning how to place an accumulator.

Bringing in the right type of senior player – one of quality and experience but also good character – therefore offered more than just some additional quality and a bit more profile for the club. A good senior group could do some of the manager's job for him, both on the pitch and in the dressing room. Steve Williams experienced that at The Dell. Thrown in as a youngster against some of the best midfielders around, he affectionately recounts:

> Ossie would seek me out after every game and say, 'That's another one you've got the better of today – keep ticking them off.' If you can't learn off Jim McCalliog, or Peter Osgood, or Ted MacDougall, you're a fool. And it grounds you. I thought I was a real player at 16 until I worked with them and realised I had miles to go. The senior players would also keep the youngsters in check, and a healthy club is made in the dressing room. If you'd been out late and they got to know of it, they wouldn't go to the manager but they'd sort you out themselves. Quite often there was no need for the manager because he'd got the dressing room right in the first place. We're talking about some very, very good footballers who passed through when I was a kid and I learned off every single one of them. Not all of it good, mind! But when you're 17 years old and want to learn about life and about football all you have to do is pick their brains really.

This was McMenemy's vision to a tee, but it wasn't always the biggest names or most expensive signings who made the biggest difference. McMenemy felt at the end of their first season in the Second Division in 1975 that he needed someone with both experience and leadership to balance the mercurial element of the team. As he was to do with Alan Ball two years later, he found that man in Peter Rodrigues. As someone Sheffield Wednesday were prepared to let go on a free transfer, who had won the last of his international caps two years previously, and who was considering retirement, not many were overexcited at the signing at the time. But Peter Osgood recognised the impact, insisting, 'Rodrigues was a masterstroke of Lawrie's.'

If McMenemy's love of the violinists meant that his teams tended to be of the 'if you score four, we'll score five' variety, Clough was clear that a successful trophy-winning machine needed to be built on defensive solidity and always looked to build a spine down the middle of his team. At Forest that took the form of Shilton – Burns – McGovern and/or Gemmill – Woodcock. McMenemy wasn't dismissive of this element either, but the truth was that he didn't quite nail it down in the manner of his friend, at least not until the arrival of Shilton and that team he built in 1984.

It's no coincidence that this team, while less flamboyant than its predecessors, came closest to securing the biggest prize. As suggested, it's something that might also explain Saints' relative lack of success in European competition compared with Ipswich and Forest, where the ability to shut out the opposition for long periods and avoid the pitfalls of the away goal made a watertight defence even more valuable. Clough not only brought in Shilton at the start of his championship-winning season but, in the same way as Robson with Hunter and Beattie, based that ultimate success on a superb central-defensive partnership. When Larry Lloyd was joined by Kenny Burns, the former felt they very quickly became as effective as any partnership in the land, and better than most. It was a foundation Clough and Robson built more effectively than McMenemy at first. All believed in attacking, entertaining football, but the first pieces of the Robson and Clough jigsaws came in defence. It was something that would make a significant difference over the next five years.

1976/77

Southampton
9th Second Division
FA Cup round 5
European Cup Winners' Cup quarter-final

Nottingham Forest
3rd Second Division – *promoted*
Anglo-Scottish Cup winners

Ipswich Town
3rd First Division

*The noise bouncing around the old wooden stands of The
Dell is as never before, McMenemy animated in the dugout
and his players winning every ball and flying forward at
every opportunity. There are still ten minutes to find the
third goal that will knock out the holders, Anderlecht, and
take Saints to a European semi-final. The momentum is
such that there is surely only one winner now. The Belgians
find one long, hopeful, and overhit ball. The March night is
as wet as the day which has preceded it and pools of water
glisten under the floodlights. Jim Steele makes to intercept
and slips in the mud. François Van der Elst buries the
ball in the bottom corner with the clinical efficiency of an
international striker and the dream is gone in an instant …*

Southampton's moment of FA Cup glory led most to assume
that the following season would be a comfortable march
to promotion. A team that had won the FA Cup and still

retained the likes of Channon, Osgood and McCalliog were too good for the second tier, surely? A home loss to newly promoted Carlisle United in the season's first match wasn't the anticipated conclusion to a day of celebratory bonhomie, and by the end of September they sat rock bottom of the table after a 6-2 defeat at Charlton. Those who felt they were too good to remain there were proved correct, as their home form dragged them out of trouble, but a mid-table finish wasn't in the plan. The season became a long seesaw between their international players failing to stir themselves for the challenges of awaydays at Millwall, Plymouth and the like, and coming to life when the big cup ties came around. Despite the vagaries and disappointment of their league form, this was a season decorated with some of the most memorable matches in which Saints have ever been involved.

Seeing off Clough's Forest in an FA Cup fourth-round replay sent them into a fifth-round tie at home to Manchester United, and the 2-2 draw, which was played out in the most febrile atmosphere imaginable and relayed on national television, was utterly compelling. Supporters were wondering whether the miracle could happen again, and the match *should* have been won. However, at Old Trafford they lost the replay and with it an FA Cup tie for the first time in nine rounds and that was the end of that particular dream.

The exotic excitement of European football also made the season special and, again, with McMenemy's rascals deciding these fixtures were worthy of their greatest attention, unprecedented things began to happen. A 4-0 home win against Olympique Marseille was a stunning start, with Peter Osgood stealing the show. By March they were in the Cup Winners' Cup quarter-final and were playing the might of Anderlecht, the holders, studded with Dutch and Belgian internationals. Having lost 2-0 in Brussels it was generally accepted that the night of 16 March at The Dell would be nothing more than a chance to see the World Cup stars while departing the tournament. However, at 2-0 up and pressing for a winner, all that was out of the window. The greatest result in The Dell's history was dangling before us. Jim Steele's defensive mistake and an away goal in the last ten minutes killed both that possibility and the atmosphere in an instant.

When combined with Old Trafford, in eight days the season had been shattered and the fans with it. But these were nights that would have been unimaginable only 12 months previously, and matches that would remain forever in Southampton folklore. Meanwhile, looking to the future, the arrival in the first team of that young midfielder named Steve Williams would prove significant.

Ipswich were proving that the previous season's high-placed finish was no fluke and developing the consistency that would see them in the top six in nine seasons out of ten. That consistency was in evidence as they won 13 and drew three of 16 consecutive matches to suggest real title ambitions. One win and four defeats in their last six matches thwarted them, leaving Liverpool to retain their title. While for once the fans didn't have European football to enjoy, as at Southampton there were moments that would linger in the memory, such as the First Division's biggest victory of the season, 7-0 against West Bromwich Albion. And the team that was to dominate Europe in 1981 was emerging, with the development of John Wark into a dangerous goalscoring midfielder, the signing and impact of Paul Mariner and the assimilation into the squad, if not yet the first team, of a young Russell Osman.

Nottingham Forest's season included the December victory in the Anglo-Scottish Cup deemed so important by their manager, but the real prize was promotion, duly achieved by a whisker in the moment of Bolton's defeat against Wolves. The team was evolving into the one that would win the league the following season, with the likes of Woodcock and Anderson emerging, Martin O'Neill and John Robertson reinvented under Clough, and crucial experienced arrivals such as Peter Withe and Larry Lloyd. Lloyd would be a particularly inspired signing, identified and acquired by Taylor when others saw little but a fading career, and a character who would fit McMenemy's idea of a rascal perfectly.

Rascals and Villains

*'When I had the King Rufus I used to have a
picture in the pub, behind the bar, of the 76 team
and I'd look at it and think to myself, "How did
he handle that lot?"'*

Peter Rodrigues,
Southampton FA Cup-winning captain

Mick Channon, Peter Osgood, Jim McCalliog, Jimmy Steele,
Charlie George, Frank Worthington, Mark Dennis, Kenny
Burns, Larry Lloyd, John Robertson, Kevin Beattie, Alan
Brazil. Not exactly a list of the foremost choirboys from
football's 70s and 80s. But what a list of talent.

In team sports there are many who have failed to manage
those supremely talented individuals of a different and
sometimes challenging character, ultimately to the detriment
of that team's chances, and with a resultant loss of enjoyment
for those who watch the game. They would be forever
concerned about the downside rather than the benefits. Talk
to Kevin Pietersen or Danny Cipriani to name but two, or
consider the maverick talents of Hudson, Currie, Bowles and
Worthington among others, and the unwillingness or inability
of England managers of the 70s to offer them a stage.

Clough, McMenemy and Robson had no such fear of
handling rascals and each did so with the hands of a master.
If they felt such characters could add to the team, they
were willing to back their own ability to manage those who

intimidated others. Sometimes there almost seemed to be an extra enjoyment in this. It was something they copyrighted, leaving other managers to rue what they had missed. This ability to take on players others were wary of handling and bring the best out of them for the betterment of the team was based simply on mutual respect.

For McMenemy such respect was certainly more forthcoming after his cup win, and it underpinned the success of these relationships and made them work. (Other than in the obvious manner, McMenemy considers the FA Cup a key moment for him as it confirmed him as a winner with the senior players.) Even in the days when Messrs Keegan, Channon and Ball were in tandem at the peak of Saints' powers, McMenemy is clear: 'There was respect on all sides, and I knew they would give me 100 per cent.' He was always confident he could handle the more flamboyant players, on and off the pitch, and was able to squeeze performances from them through which they earned his respect. In turn, their gratitude to and respect for him also grew.

Having handled the Paine issue on arrival, by the time Rodrigues joined the following year any significant challenges to McMenemy's authority had come and gone. Rodrigues says, 'From the time I arrived I don't recall anyone disrespecting Lawrie, even if he did have to build his credibility with the likes of Mick [Channon].' And Channon himself confirms that while he always liked Lawrie, it was the major trophy that cemented that true respect from the international stars. Certainly, after leaving in 1977 for Manchester City, it was a very different and more commanding McMenemy he found upon his return two years later. Channon subsequently began referring to his manager as 'The Ayatollah'.

The ability to rejuvenate such players by getting something more from them was evident in Clough. When you listen to Kenny Burns, Larry Lloyd or John Robertson on their time under him at Forest, each was given a new lease of life by his management, and each returned that favour with trophy after trophy. They may have been powerful characters, but John McGovern watched their assimilation into the team, sometimes in roles they weren't expecting, and it worked because 'they listened out of respect'.

There were still lines to be drawn, with McMenemy saying he would always sign a rascal if he could play but not a villain, even if he was a better player. The importance of the distinction meant that McMenemy put a lot of store in checking a player's personal and family life and his vices before making a decision, as did Clough and Robson. When looking to sign Colin Todd in 1978, he would say, 'I knew what he could do but I didn't know much about what kind of a person he was off the field. It is essential to know that.'

Alan Ball may have been drawn to Southampton to be with his horse-racing mates Channon and Osgood and was quite capable of holding his own in the good-time stakes. Whether that qualified him as a rascal, given he was one of the most genuine and passionate players of his generation, loved by all then and now, is debatable but McMenemy had no evidence of his own for this before he first signed him. Therefore, even someone as 'solid gold' as Bally would get the investigative treatment in advance.

Such surveillance work was something Clough and Taylor also made a non-negotiable at Forest when considering signings. Taylor went private detective in his determination to know everything about a player's background and they, like McMenemy, took on board the rough diamonds, but never those they would consider the shysters. Clough would say, 'If there was something to be known about a player – something he preferred to hide – you could count on us finding out. Such information can be priceless.'

In terms of sorting the rascals from the villains, it was indeed. Nick Holmes saw McMenemy as a shrewd judge of character, which allowed him to bring in star names without any adverse effect on a harmonious dressing room. On the contrary, many of the rascals brought in made the positive spirit what it was. Shrewd was a word used by many players when discussing the managers and their most influential characteristics. McMenemy, in particular, was shrewd, both as a man and a manager. When he considered the secret of his mate Clough's success, he came to a conclusion that could equally have been applied to himself. It was simply that he knew how to deal with players. Crucially, it wasn't important to be liked, but essential to be respected. Mick Channon showed some of that respect when he said, 'It speaks volumes for the man that he had the courage to try to tame this wild bunch he had hand-picked for himself. His balancing act was worth its place in any circus.'

Russell Osman explained how the Ipswich players also understood this hierarchy when it came to the manager being liked and respected, and that the respect ultimately came from honesty, trust and the application of common sense: 'You can't go through a long managerial career without falling out with people and we were strong characters. But a key thing about Bobby and his management of players like us was that he didn't hold a grudge. A lot of us went on to be managers and we definitely took his qualities with us.'

Might this ability to integrate and maximise the talent of such characters mean accusations of double standards in man-management? McMenemy was comfortable that 'you don't impose stupid restrictions on exceptional players. They are men and my job was to make them feel responsible for their own well-being', and Nick Holmes saw at first-hand in the Saints' dressing room that McMenemy 'learned to make allowances', much like Alex Ferguson's handling of Eric Cantona. The United manager's players were aware Cantona sometimes lived by different rules, but like their manager they weren't going to rock the boat while the genius was helping to deliver success.

Peter Osgood recalled how important it was to him that McMenemy insisted that he would revolutionise the club from top to bottom, but he wouldn't try to change him – that flair should be nourished, not blunted. When McMenemy brought Charlie George to the club in December 1978 eyebrows were raised, with George being seen by many in the game as more villain than rascal. McMenemy felt differently and knew he could get something from what was still an extremely talented player. In *The Diary of a Season* McMenemy's co-writer Brian Scovell introduced a chapter on the pursuit and signing of George, in a way that reinforced the effect these managers could have on players of a certain character: 'George was controversial in his behaviour and that made some managers wary of him. That made him McMenemy's type of player. Charlie had been a rebel, but marriage and parenthood had matured him. His career was ready for a good manager to exploit.'

Good managers did indeed exploit such talent and used their antennae for assessing the mood and the right moment to crack the whip or play along. Osgood recounted a tale of a day after training during Saints' promotion season, with things going well, when he and Ball decided it was worth sharing a bottle of champagne in the sauna. Someone let on to McMenemy ... who promptly arrived with his own bottle and, fully suited and booted, joined them to share a drink on the 'if you can't beat 'em, join 'em' principle. The fact that the story was told a quarter of a century after it happened suggests the manager had made the right impression and hit the right note.

This practicality – that as managers they saw no point in cutting off their nose to spite their face and sacrificing free spirits completely on the altar of perceived discipline – is exemplified by John Wark's recollection of some high jinks at Ipswich:

We played Saint-Étienne away in that famous game in the quarter-final of the UEFA Cup and Bobby gave us the afternoon off the day before the game. A group of us went into the town and had a few. We were spotted and when we got back to the hotel Bobby was waiting and said, 'You're all fined two weeks wages.' We thought, *Shit, what's going to happen here?* They scored after 15 minutes and then we murdered them – Johnny Rep and all – and won 4-1. As we came into the dressing room Bobby said, 'And you can forget the fine lads.' He'd made the point but not flogged it.

Such an ability to read a moment and react in the way most conducive to both discipline and team spirit was valuable, even if it meant employing a flexible approach and a certain degree of amateur psychology.

They wanted proven talent and McMenemy, in particular, would look for this dash of flair to complete his teams. When he sensed in the pursuit of Charlie George that there was less enthusiasm among his directors for this big-name signing than that of Osgood five years previously, some thinking he might cause upset at the club, he pushed for their support and reaffirmed his enjoyment in adding a bit of spice, telling them, 'When I came here this club had so many gangsters that Al Capone would've struggled to get a game but I sorted it out. We need someone with a bit of flair and excitement otherwise we'll be called the Saints convent team.'

From the outside, McMenemy's acquisition of Osgood was also felt to come with issues attached. With his love of the finer things in life, as well as the horses (the wisdom of uniting him in a dressing room with Mick Channon, and later Alan Ball, was therefore seen as questionable), many felt he was coming south for a gentle retirement and continued easy access to Windsor, Ascot and Newbury. (The coaching staff at The Dell in the days of Channon, Brian O'Neill, McCalliog, Ball and Osgood would always know on which days there was a meeting at one of these venues, partly due to the enthusiasm and speed with which this group would aim to get through the allotted drills, but mainly because on walking through the dressing room once the players were out training, hanging from at least five pegs would be not boots or other footballing paraphernalia, but pairs of binoculars.) But on Osgood, McMenemy was adamant. To him the supposed 'big-time Charlie' was rarely any trouble at all.

The stunts the rascals pulled were good-humoured if sometimes intoxicated pranks that differentiated them from villains and contributed to the fun and togetherness. Maybe it helped that it was a different time, when the rascals were embraced for their escapades rather than being hung out to dry by media and administrators alike for bringing the game into disrepute. Osgood commandeered the FA Cup and took it for a night-long joyride, while Tony Woodcock revealed that he and John Robertson did similar, and perhaps could be considered to have gone one better, with the European Cup: 'We took the cup to my dad's work – Robbo and myself – and we put it in the back of my sponsored car. On the way back Robbo suggested a couple of beers, which was far from out of character. So, we parked in the car park with the cup in the boot – or that was the plan ... the boot wouldn't close so we left it on the back seat with a blanket over it and forgot about it for two hours.' What was it with hijacking trophies? Still, the rascals could hardly be disciplined for such larceny, least of all at Ipswich, given their manager took his precious FA Cup home with him in 1978 and slept with it all night. Happy days.

If divisiveness driven by over-inflated egos was the trait in villains the managers wanted to avoid, the most recent justification of that as a policy might be seen in the disintegration and regeneration of Manchester United in 2022/23. Erik ten Hag managed to rebuild a shattered culture at the club, with immediate results on the pitch, in a manner reminiscent of those challenges faced down by our three managers in the early 70s. Having dispensed with the likes of

Lukaku, Pogba and Ronaldo, United set about a new approach for future signings. It's believed that the only contribution to the strategy made by the chief executive, Richard Arnold, was a succinct and sensible 'no dickheads'.

As a two-word summary of the strategy of McMenemy, Robson and Clough when it came to signings, that will do nicely.

1977/78

Southampton
2nd Second Division – *promoted*

Nottingham Forest
LEAGUE CHAMPIONS
LEAGUE CUP WINNERS
FA Cup quarter-final
Football Writers' Player of the Year – Kenny Burns
PFA Player of the Year – Peter Shilton
PFA Young Player of the Year – Tony Woodcock

Ipswich Town
18th First Division
FA CUP WINNERS
UEFA Cup round 3

Ian Wallace's hooked cross floats over Kenny Burns and Larry Lloyd and arrives on the head of his reliable and powerful strike partner Mick Ferguson. He's three yards from goal and unmarked. He meets the ball powerfully … and Peter Shilton finds the save of the season, of many seasons, to somehow flick it over the bar. Shilton has been keeping clean sheets all season. This one, 0-0, gives a special sheen to a sunny spring afternoon in the West Midlands – the sort on which football supporters sense the coming of the summer and the close of the season. Nottingham Forest have just won the league championship.

* * *

Nineteen-year-old David Geddis has had little chance to contribute to Ipswich's season. He finds himself a relative unknown in the television build-up to the FA Cup Final, owing his place to Trevor Whymark's injury. Now he's playing the match of his life. On a classic cup final Saturday the temperature is heading towards 100 degrees on the pitch in the airless cauldron of Wembley. Ipswich are taking Arsenal apart, but Mariner hits the bar in front of an open goal and John Wark arrows thunderbolts against the same goalpost twice in the second half. A sense of unease is growing that this could be turning into an underdog's hard luck story. 'What have we to do?' are the words David Coleman suggests might be accompanying Bobby Robson's gesture at the blue sky above, as if his misfortune is the fault not of Mariner but of some greater force. Just 13 minutes left and now Geddis turns Nelson inside out on the right wing. His cutback is half stopped by Young but Roger Osborne, as unlikely a hero as Bobby Stokes two years before him, drives the ball into the net. The emotion of the moment and the heat of the day remove Osborne from the action immediately but if he never played another minute for Ipswich, he would reside in their history forever. He'd won Ipswich Town the FA Cup.

This was the season in which all three clubs delivered, and in terms of pure success was the pinnacle when considered as a combined set of achievements.

Ipswich's league form deserted them, finishing two places above the relegation zone in 18th. Few will remember or worry about that given the day they gave their town and supporters on Saturday, 6 May at Wembley, bringing home the FA Cup to their 'sleepy backwater' for the first and only time in their history, matching Southampton two years before them. The parallels were many and various – not least the scorching weather, which seemed somehow to add to the iconic nature of the day. Ipswich's chances were dismissed as Saints' had been before them, with the Arsenal team of Brady, Hudson and Malcolm Macdonald the clear favourites. (Supermac was one of those confidently holding and sharing that opinion, if memory serves correctly.) But, like Southampton, the Ipswich players and manager had every confidence that their togetherness would win the day. 'Nobody gave us a chance,' recalled Robson. It meant everything to the players to prove people wrong and to get some major silverware at last to supplement the plaudits they had received for the previous five years.

Back in Europe, Ipswich may not have progressed past the third round – but that third round will forever be another magic moment. To see the world's best player, Johan Cruyff, at Portman Road with Barcelona and then see Ipswich win 3-0 was a gobsmacking statement of how far they had come. The heartbreak of losing the tie on a penalty shoot-out at the Camp Nou was real, but the fact that the club were now regular visitors to such iconic stadiums filled the townspeople with a mixture of pride and astonishment. And all the while the team of 81 continued to build, with the significant debuts during the season of Alan Brazil and Terry Butcher.

Although the FA Cup remained the highest-profile domestic club trophy in world football, and many fans prioritised it over the league, Nottingham Forest must be considered to have gone one better by winning the league championship in their first season back in the top tier. Today it is, of course, considered by far the more significant achievement. Winning 11 of their first 14 matches wasn't enough to convince their rivals that they were serious contenders and was deemed, correctly, to have been aided by the element of surprise. That began to change on 17 December when Forest produced a display of simple but devastating efficiency in beating

Manchester United 4-0 at Old Trafford, inflicting their joint-heaviest home defeat in the league since 1959.

The number still harbouring doubts reduced further when, on 22 March, Forest won their first major trophy under Clough, their first in 29 years, by beating their nearest title rivals, the might of European champions Liverpool, in a League Cup Final replay. To play for three and a half hours in a final against Liverpool and not concede a goal was a signpost to the defensive foundations that were to deliver major trophies for the next three years. The season saw three signings critical to this success and those to come: Peter Shilton, Kenny Burns and Archie Gemmill. Shilton finished the season as the PFA Player of the Year, while Tony Woodcock's Young Player of the Year award was concrete evidence of Clough's ability to make the players he had inherited so much better.

Southampton's achievement was less exalted but significant in their progress to becoming one of the teams of the early 80s. McMenemy had seen the need to dismantle his cup winners and rebuild a more pragmatic but consistent team if he was to get out of the Second Division. He offset the by-now-inevitable departure of Mick Channon with the shrewd acquisition of proven First Division performers Chris Nicholl and Phil Boyer, who would contribute 19 league goals, and promotion was confirmed at home to Tottenham on the last day of the season.

A season of success for all three clubs. Success delivered by the shared belief in simplicity.

A Simple Game

'Great leaders are almost always great simplifiers.'

Colin Powell, former US Secretary of State

'There was no plan. It was "this is the ball ...
pass it to a team-mate".'

Viv Anderson, Nottingham Forest

'The hardest thing in football is to play simple. He insisted we keep it simple. Everyone knew what their role was – there was no other tactical stuff.' So says Tony Woodcock of the approach that made Forest pre-eminent in domestic and European football.

The managers had developed their own beliefs about the way the game should be played and had come to the same conclusions. They were adamant it was a game to be played on the ground. Robson's adherence to this had its origins in watching the Hungarians of the 1950s, who took England to the cleaners twice in a year, and the 'push and run' team developed under Arthur Rowley at Tottenham. Secondly, all three felt that too many people over-complicated things and that simplicity should underpin everything they did. None was a disciple of Charles Hughes and the FA coaching manual's statistics-led approach for 'effective' football. 'It wasn't my way of playing. I liked the beautiful game, the passing game,' said Robson, who, in common with Clough, felt successful football pretty much began and ended with being able to pass the ball

151

to a player on the same team in a decent position. He may have been influenced initially by Rowley and Puskás, but he wasn't beyond admiring Clough's Forest either: 'Forest's football was lovely on the eye. I used to like watching them because they played carpet football, all on the ground, constructive football.' Simplicity of instruction and passing the ball took precedence over spending a long time trying to improve individual technique.

Allan Hunter is once again to the point: 'Simplicity was the word, I think.' Russell Osman agrees:

> Bobby was very good at getting the basics right; 90 per cent of what we did on the training ground was about making sure you were passing the ball as well as possible with an appreciation of the player on the other end of it. He saw that as the foundation for everything. It was as simple as 'pass it to someone with the same-coloured shirt on'.

For Robson, read Clough. Perhaps if Charlie Hughes had attended *their* coaching sessions rather than the other way round, England and the FA might not have gone as long as 16 years without reaching even a quarter-final.

That said, Osman is insistent that at Ipswich there was an important facilitator of the simplicity – to pass and move for 90 minutes in as many matches as it took to challenge for a treble with a 14-man first-team squad, you couldn't be a carthorse: 'What people didn't give us credit for was how fit we were. We played over 60 games in 80/81, all at full tilt.' It was, though, fitness for football and a certain type of football, which came almost organically with the demands of that style, and a ball was very much a part of any fitness regime.

However, simplicity based on passing wasn't merely for the purpose of keeping the ball. Possession for the sake of the Opta statisticians wasn't deemed the holy grail it appears to be today. It had to have a purpose. The clinical effectiveness of these teams' passing games was based on passing the ball *forward*. Robson himself said, 'It wasn't nice passing for the sake of it … I look at Premier League players passing the ball square, without looking, and think, "Hang on, the idea is to play the ball forward."' And Clough worked on the simple principle that if you weren't getting the ball in the direction of the goal you were unlikely to score many. Woodcock tells a story that reinforces the principles of simplicity of action and clarity of instruction. Asking Clough what the plans were for free kicks, he replied, 'Shoot.' But what if it was an indirect free kick? 'Tap it to one side and shoot.'

There was also a shared liking for getting the ball to the byline and cutting it back. Clough built two championship-winning teams on the back of Alan Hinton and John Robertson beating a man and crossing the ball. It may sound obvious but consider how rarely it happens in today's game, where wingers play on the 'wrong' side to cut back in at every turn, and full-backs play as additional midfielders rather than overlappers in the manner of a Burley, a Golac or a Viv Anderson. David Geddis to Roger Osborne, FA Cup Final 1978, Robertson to Trevor Francis, European Cup Final 1979 – so many of the goals that mattered were created this way. Not complicated, simply effective and, with the right players, remarkably difficult to stop.

The former Tottenham manager Tim Sherwood talks of his irritation today with what he sees as the contrived nonsense of pie charts and analysis employed by so many modern managers, especially when pitching for a job. He's scornful of the amount of time spent peering at laptops and even drawing pictures on iPads for players at the side of the pitch mid-game. Talk of 'false nines' and 'transitions' he sees as bunkum, suggesting coaches should concentrate on spending time with their players face to face. Our managers would have agreed wholeheartedly. The image of Clough presenting anybody with a pie chart to illustrate how he planned to create trophy winners is one to store up for a rainy day when something is required to put a smile back on one's face.

This doctrine of simplicity was not only applied to how their own teams played. To avoid over-complication there was not a lot that focused on tactics, and particularly not in relation to adapting the approach for different opposition. Clough was certainly not one for such things and believed a lot of over-thought nonsense populated traditional coaching. The mention of that name of Charlie Hughes was likely to get Clough's back up even more swiftly than that of his latest chairman. What the opposition were up to didn't concern Clough – if his team did their thing it would work regardless. Similarly, at Ipswich, John Wark says, 'The opposition became irrelevant because we all felt that if we played our game well, we could beat anybody,' although Russell Osman hints at additional challenges in analysing other teams that came with their manager's idiosyncrasies and famous struggles with names: 'Bobby would call Emlyn Hughes "Elwyn", and Watford's striker was always "Bluther Lissett." So, funnily enough, we didn't do a whole lot on the opposition for fear of dying of laughter.'

It was also a matter of horses for courses. McMenemy's training at lower division clubs would concentrate more on the physical, but his view was that once you were working with thoroughbreds with the talent of Ball, Channon and Osgood you had to do much less of that and instead he would get the ball out, play football and do things they loved doing and *were good at*, focusing on a player's strengths, ensuring that the other parts of the jigsaw covered any weaknesses.

Too much focus on the opposition and stopping them playing was too negative a mindset and, notwithstanding the occasional tactical tweak such as that man-marking of Tony Currie in the League Cup semi-final, Steve Williams recalls McMenemy pointing out the downside to him after the 1979

League Cup Final. Williams felt he had 'done a job' on Archie Gemmill and the Forest midfielder had a poor game by his standards. McMenemy suggested to Williams that he had actually been below par too – because although he had stopped Gemmill playing, in doing so he hadn't played himself, and as his most creative midfielder that had cost the team. Williams felt he learned a lesson that day.

Viv Anderson offers a succinct summation of Clough's playing philosophy: 'It was simplicity, not over-complication, well communicated. This was the genius.' Anderson calls it genius, although neither Clough nor Robson nor McMenemy probably saw it that way. To them it was just common sense. And it worked.

1978/79

Southampton
14th First Division
League Cup runners-up
FA Cup quarter-final

Nottingham Forest
Runners-up First Division
LEAGUE CUP WINNERS
FA Cup round 5
EUROPEAN CUP WINNERS

Ipswich Town
6th First Division
FA Cup quarter-final
European Cup Winners' Cup quarter-final

*'It's very nearly unbearable to watch, never mind to play in,'
a breathless Barry Davies suggests in commentary. There
are just minutes to go in Cologne and Forest lead through
Ian Bowyer's second-half header. Shilton flies to his left to
keep out another effort, which would have seen them out at
the semi-final stage on away goals. Then the final whistle
and Davies's relief: 'And Nottingham Forest are in the
European Cup Final ... and they've done it the hard way.'
After the chaos of the 3–3 first leg and the assumption their
goose was cooked, the only man not in the least perturbed
was Clough. As he had proven through four successive cup
ties against Liverpool in which his team conceded not a*

single goal, this sort of assignment was Forest's forte, built on togetherness, simplicity and belief.

Seven weeks on and Davies is at the microphone again as John Robertson beats his man and puts the ball on Trevor Francis's head in first-half injury time of a non-event of a European Cup Final up to that point. Francis nods the ball into the roof of the net. 'Well, that's what I've wanted to see Robertson do!' The implication that he might have been better employed on the Forest bench than in the commentary box may have been a rather sweet moment of excited impertinence from Barry but few people in Nottingham, away from Meadow Lane, cared. They stood looking down on the rest of Europe.

The season of 1978/79 would confirm that Southampton could hold their own in the First Division and, with the help of The Dell, always be a threat in the cups; that Ipswich could hold their own domestically and abroad; and that Nottingham Forest could more than hold their own and had been moulded into one of the finest teams in Europe.

Confounding those who saw the previous season as an anomaly, Forest defended their title tenaciously before bending the knee to a Liverpool team that conceded only 14 goals all season. In the process they extended their unbeaten run in the league to an unprecedented 42 matches. Some flash in the pan. But the trophies were to keep coming. The retention of their League Cup, beating McMenemy's Southampton in the Wembley final, was impressive but no longer to be considered a surprise. The conquering of Europe via the European Cup win was something else entirely. From the moment they produced a two-leg masterclass at their first attempt to overcome the holders Liverpool in round one, Clough's ambition to finally lift the trophy after, as far as he was concerned, being robbed of it when at Derby was heightened. That away win in Cologne in the second leg of the semi-final, when most assumed they were out, was classic Forest – classic Clough and Taylor – and by the time Clough had finished telling them how it would pan out, nobody at the club was in any doubt they would prevail.

For once, Clough and Taylor used the finances they had generated through success to bring in a star name – the first-ever million-pound footballer in Britain – Trevor Francis. This was a departure from the normal route of polishing rough diamonds at basement prices – one that would come back to bite them when they overindulged their taste for such big statements over the following seasons. But for now, Europe had completed the Clough miracle. Four and a half years from rusting tugboat to European champions.

Ipswich had more adventures in Europe, this time in the Cup Winners' Cup. Again, they made the third round; again, they came up against Barcelona. The formula was the same – an epic European night at Portman Road as they beat the European giants once more, but a narrow defeat away, and this time elimination on away goals. Eleven days before that defeat their misfortune with cup draws had them facing Liverpool in their defence of the FA Cup. A 1-0 home defeat meant that, much in the manner of Saints two years previously, a season of huge promise was over in the blink of an eye. Once again Robson added an important part of the 1981 jigsaw, signing Dutchman Arnold Mühren at the start of the season in a deal that would pay back in spades.

Southampton's return to the First Division was accompanied by a couple of signings that were pure McMenemy – he joined the fashion for overseas signings after the Argentina World Cup, bringing in the attacking Yugoslav right-back Ivan Golac, whose cavalier style was to be the embodiment of the Saints' approach in the coming years, for good and for bad. Midway through the season, looking for that bit of stardust that had been lacking since losing Channon and Osgood, McMenemy courted Charlie George, one of the original mavericks who bestrode the game in the early 70s, in a protracted transfer saga that was settled by the power of the manager's own personality. He had secured himself another of his rascals but was in no doubt he had the ability to manage him.

A Degree in People

'Before you are a leader, success is all about growing yourself. When you become a leader, success is all about growing others.'

Jack Welch, former CEO, General Electric Company

When someone mentioned the name of Mike Brearley to the former Australian fast bowler Rodney Hogg, he asked, 'Isn't that the guy with a degree in people?' Brearley was the England cricket captain in the late 70s and early 80s and an extremely successful one. His own playing abilities were questioned when assessing his worthiness of a place in the team but he built a reputation for managing his players, including the strongest and most sensitive characters, that superseded this achievement gap and created a tight team so used to winning that his own low scores were almost irrelevant. A sort of cricketing McMenemy perhaps. John Arlott considered that Test cricket never had a better captain 'strategically, tactically, above all, in psychological perception and handling of men'.

In Brearley's case, this description was given credence by his training, and then future career, in psychoanalysis. Our managers had no such qualifications or any desire for them. As Clough said inimitably when asked whether psychology was important in management, 'Ask Sigmund Freud how many European Cups he won …'

These managers had done their own growing and were now ready to grow others. Talk to those who worked with them or witnessed their success and they consistently refer, in all three cases, to a brilliance at man-management. Regarding Clough specifically, John McGovern is succinct, saying simply, 'He *was* man-management.'

Are man-management and coaching distinct or are they actually the same thing? Football coaching in the conventional sense within the game was something managers were purveying up and down the country, inevitably with varying degrees of success. With McMenemy, Clough and Robson the coaching was not of the sort that was deemed conventional and was wrapped up within their man-management approach. What set them apart were their 'degrees in people'. There's more than one way of making players, and therefore teams, better, and by seeing coaching as something more than cones and tactics boards and two hours a day on the training ground they shared a highly effective method of doing so.

Even so, they prided themselves that they had learned the game thoroughly. In the cases of Clough and Robson this came, in part, from rising to international quality as players themselves, but all three would acknowledge they had also been well schooled in how the game should be played most effectively. McMenemy recalls his mentor at Sheffield Wednesday, Alan Brown, as a coach ahead of his time, his advocacy of exemplary coaching, always up to date or in front of the game, and how he insisted his staff take coaching courses at Lilleshall and meet and talk with other coaches whenever possible to spark new ideas that might offer an advantage. It's unlikely, therefore, that McMenemy would welcome being considered a manager at the expense of being an effective coach, even though his cup-winning skipper's own experience was that 'he was more man-manager than coach'.

McMenemy suggests that the fact he was the first in England to introduce and consistently use the continental-style sweeper system, on which the success of his 1984 team was built, is evidence of the fact that he could coach technically when he needed to. His skill may have been perceived primarily as a man-manager, but in the opinion of journalist Bob Harris, who knew him as well as any at this time, 'He knew the game inside out.' Steve Williams comes down on the same side as Rodrigues on this:

> They weren't great coaches in my eyes, they were great managers. At Saints, Lew Chatterley did most of the football coaching. When I went to Arsenal, Don Howe was a great coach but an awful manager. If there was a team to pick he'd pick the wrong one – in fact he'd ask me what I thought it should be. That's not great management. Then George Graham followed him and we were back to good manager who didn't really coach, and he sorted things out within six weeks. Look who had the success. So coaching can be delegated but I'm not sure great man-management can be.

All three could undoubtedly hold their own on a training pitch. Robson saw striker Alan Brazil as hugely talented when he arrived at Ipswich, with a wonderful left foot, but he also felt he didn't know where to run, couldn't head the ball and maybe lacked the hard-working ingredient. He was insistent that Ipswich made Brazil a great player. His future England captain Terry Butcher insists Robson was miles ahead of his time, but many of their players would say they weren't coached much in the currently accepted sense of the word. Russell Osman says of Robson, 'It was really just about standards – on the pitch as well as off. Tactically we didn't really do anything. For Bobby that maybe came later in his career, particularly in his jobs in Europe. But not with us.'

Clough was no more interested in tactics than he was in board meetings. Tony Woodcock says, 'It was different when I went to Cologne, where you worked on skills and tactics. We didn't have any tactics. But he knew the game enough to tweak to good effect.' It's notable that both Woodcock and Osman refer to the difference in the European approach. For all the much-vaunted tactical sophistication of the European teams as opposed to the simplicity preached by Clough and Robson, it was six years after Woodcock moved to the continent before a non-English team won a European Cup.

It's too simplistic to consider Clough as nothing but a man-manager; he *did* coach but apparently without anybody realising it while it was happening. His philosophy was 'less is more' and his fondness for strolling into training with his dog halfway through the session may have seemed like laziness but it was nothing of the sort, rather a deliberate act. McMenemy would occasionally walk round with him at his training sessions (another throwback that would be a back-page headline today) and recalled how training would immediately intensify on his appearance without him saying a word.

The automatic assumption is that making players better comes from technical coaching and repeated skills training aimed at improving the individual. This wasn't their way. They believed that players at that level, especially once they had been identified as the right ones for the job the managers had in mind and advised where they fitted in the jigsaw, should be good enough to be trusted to perform. It was less about making them *better* than making them more *effective*. They had an ability to spot a kernel of talent in the most unlikely outer casings – perhaps the clearest example being Clough's perseverance with a player who on first acquaintance struck him as an absolute slob. But Clough knew that if a manager looked hard enough, he may find talent that others couldn't see. Is that not a coaching skill in itself? At clubs where the purse strings mattered this was a priceless ability. John Robertson would become the most effective winger in Europe, even if Clough was never entirely convinced that he had eliminated all traces of the slob. In truth that didn't matter if the player was working hard for him and could deliver for him on the pitch. Steve Williams sees this ability to get something from a player that others couldn't as more important than coaching in these success stories: 'John Robertson – it was because Clough *saw* something there. And that's how they did it.'

They concentrated on identifying where a player's strengths lay, and ensuring those strengths were utilised as effectively as possible within the team structure, rather than spending time working on things the player couldn't do. If that player couldn't do it, there would be someone else who could. McGovern told me that Clough believed players at that level should have ability anyway and 'what he wanted to add was to develop their dedication and character'. And acquiring that character was a prerequisite if you wanted to play for any of these managers for any length of time.

Tony Woodcock suggests:

> With Brian it was all about character – he wanted you tough. And basically, if you could handle a relationship with Cloughie, you could certainly handle anything on the pitch. He understood that and it's why he managed the way he did and it's why, ultimately, we had no fear of having to go and win in Cologne or Berlin, behind the Iron Curtain. We could play anywhere, against anybody. We had character. Once we had that we could win in any way – play it on the floor or mix it if we had to.

It's a quality Allan Hunter refers to in Robson's Ipswich too. These teams could be pretty, but they weren't going to be pushed around. And any Southampton team containing the likes of Jim Steele or Mark Dennis was scarcely one to take on. There was steel, mental and physical, allied to the skill.

All the players interviewed for this book felt they became better players in their time at the clubs but confirmed it was rarely through classic coaching, rather getting them to do a job in a way that best suited their talents and with absolute *clarity* as to what was expected of them, and then – critically – letting them get on with it and *trusting* them to perform and letting them know they knew that they would. This in turn built that player's confidence – the manager's belief in them was self-perpetuating – and improved their contribution to the team and to success. Players refer to subtle or almost subliminal instruction, which made a difference, without them ever needing to know why or how. And that approach wasn't just relevant for the young, developing players, as Mick Channon confirms: 'Lawrie had this gift of taking experienced players and squeezing them … still managing to find some juice in the old arses even after they should've dried up.'

Clough famously signed the uncompromising Scottish centre-forward Kenny Burns ('Kenneth' to Clough) from Birmingham after promotion to the First Division. To everyone's bemusement, not least Burns's, Clough installed him in the team at centre-half. He didn't ever feel the need to explain himself – John McGovern saw the transformation and advises that Clough never once explained to Burns why he was playing where he was playing. By the end of his first season under Clough, and his first-ever in his new position, Burns was voted Footballer of the Year. That was the only explanation Clough believed was required.

This ability to assess potential strengths and to feed them more effectively into a clear role in the team is apparent when you consider five players who were already at the City Ground when Clough arrived and weren't showing much potential to lift Forest from their Second Division mid-table stupor. Viv Anderson, John Robertson, Ian Bowyer, Martin O'Neill and Tony Woodcock were European Cup winners fewer than four years later, four of them becoming internationals and playing at World Cups. It was what Duncan Hamilton referred to in the case of Clough as the ability 'to make the ordinary extraordinary'. Small wonder there's still both awe and affection for the man from those players today.

A couple of stories illustrate the effectiveness of the subtle approach. Russell Osman recalls a match at Manchester City:

> Bobby would say, 'Why can't you play more like Bobby Moore?' Easier said than done, I reckoned. He said I was forever charging in, tackling, and I should watch footage of Moore and learn something. We won at Man City a few games later and I came in feeling I'd barely broken sweat. I thought I was in for a bollocking. Instead, Bobby said, 'That's the way to play.' I reckoned I hadn't done anything all game and he said, 'That's because you didn't have to – you read the game, you were in the right place at the right time and you made interceptions, not tackles.' And you realised he was right. Was that *coaching*? Possibly, but it was certainly good management.

Tony Woodcock's experience with Clough was similar:

> Cloughie never told me how to play tactically. In all my years with him he only once asked me to do something different. He said, 'I'd like you to play a little more on the right tonight – not completely, but just keep it in your mind to be right side.' The game? The first leg of our European Cup tie against Liverpool when we knocked out the holders and then went on to win it. If you watch our two goals – the only two of the tie – they both come from me putting the ball in from that position. He never said why, but I looked at it afterwards and realised he was smart. The other thing I remember was when our coach, Jimmy Gordon, was trying to get me to move away from defenders and I said, 'No, I want to be touch tight with him so I know

where he is, and I can turn him.' Cloughie overheard and came down on my side: 'Good answer, young man – I was a goalscorer and that's what I wanted.' And that's about as far as coaching went. A couple of subtle comments but both made a difference. It wasn't made a big deal – just economy of words and effort.

In one of Clough's more famous responses, to a journalist asking him a question on coaching, he evidenced both his belief in certain standards and his valuing of simplicity in all things coaching: 'Me telling Roy McFarland to get his haircut, now that's high-class coaching.'

It's interesting to consider how many of the players who improved by their own admission under these managers progressed to greater heights after they left. Not many. John Wark with Liverpool, arguably; Mark Wright continued his journey to high-class England centre-half; Tony Woodcock was one of a select few who made the decision, and a success of the decision, to broaden his football education abroad. But others? Mick Channon? Steve Williams? Danny Wallace? Steve Moran? Paul Mariner? Garry Birtles? Alan Brazil? John Robertson? Martin O'Neill? Trevor Francis? All were vital to the success of their clubs and produced their best football under these managers and couldn't exercise that same level of influence elsewhere. This was surely proof that their managers had a shared talent for understanding better than anyone else how to coax the very best out of people.

Tim Smith cites the number of Ipswich players he followed who were at the 1982 World Cup: Burley, Mills, Butcher, Wark, Brazil, Mariner. Osman must have missed out by a whisker and Mühren and Thijssen would assuredly have been there too if their own nation had qualified. Over the decade this was another source of pride for managers and fans alike. I recall the excitement of Mick Channon being the only England player at the club when I attended my first match in 1975. But that was it. Ipswich's David Johnson had his moment with England around the same time, but the Saints, Ipswich and Forest squads were barely touched when it came to international squad announcement time. Not for long. To be fair, the fact Saints ended up having six England captains in their ranks over this period was more to do with signings, but the likes of Steve Williams and Danny Wallace developed from the youth system to England international level.

There was a balance employed that was integral to the degree in people – an ability to empathise and to put an arm around a shoulder when it would benefit the team, but to keep a distance between players and manager that wouldn't compromise authority or the ability to take the tough decision. McMenemy felt this was important – he believed a manager shouldn't love his players too much, if at all, which was also something Clough lived by. Clough was a mass of contradictions in the way he interacted with people, including his players, often just depending on his mood. He did, however, have a fascinating, possibly unique, ability to be aggressive, rude and loved all at the same time. His friend McMenemy saw a man of quirky eccentricity who could be embarrassingly brusque with others, and yet 'the same people would be drawn to him like a magnet'. That unpredictability would fuel his effectiveness and his ability to motivate.

Woodcock acknowledges that there was discipline but 'then again, that could change in an instant and it would be "go and get your passports, we're off to Majorca". It kept us on our toes and guessing, which is the way Cloughie wanted it.' As with McMenemy, it wasn't always fire and brimstone; he could do empathy and support as well as anyone if the mood took him and he could see the potential benefit. He insisted that the way Peter Taylor boosted him in his playing days was a lesson he took with him and tried to apply to his own players: 'I've tried to do the same for my players. Irrespective of their ability you'd be staggered at how much they need a reassuring little lift at various stages of their careers.' Although Martin O'Neill may have read that passage with a half-raised eyebrow, he himself eventually felt the power contained in just a word of support from Clough.

On TalkSPORT, Stuart Pearce, who spent eight years under Clough at Forest, explained that he would man-manage by taking a contrary position, and it wasn't always rule by fear:

> It was different every day. He brought simplicity and the main thing was respect. But he knew exactly how to play it at the right times. If you were doing well, he'd cut you down without doubt – if you'd been away with England and so on. He could belittle you. But if anyone was struggling, he would be incredibly supportive if he believed in you. There were times at the City Ground when the crowd might get on the back of a certain player and Cloughie would charge out of his dugout and let them know in no uncertain terms that they should shut up. 'I believe in this lad so get behind him.'

Tony Woodcock has a similar recollection of Clough's motivational methods. 'Compliments would come in a certain way, designed to keep you grounded. He wouldn't ever say, "You played well," but he might say, "Young man, you were a credit to the game today." And the methods and the man meant such a comment was worth breaking your back for.'

But Clough wasn't one to bend his approach based on the specific personality in front of him. McGovern is adamant he never changed for anybody. This is why, even now, Clough's players' accounts of their time with him portray wildly different experiences, but based on *their* varied characters, not his. Brian Clough didn't change to accommodate them – they each had to find their own way to deal with it. He brooked little argument. He would find a way to do things differently. McGovern recalls how 'sometimes he would be rollicking me, but it was actually for the benefit of the bloke next to me because he knew I could take it'. He turned doing what was least expected of him into a fine art with indisputable results, ensuring his execution was the equal of his innovation. He made both friends and enemies but, while he often lacked tact, he infused an immense drive and energy into his club and his players.

Clough understood that being sparing to the point of complete denial with any praise was a valuable tool in getting the best from certain characters in his squad, who became so desperate for his affirmation that they would strive for it as never before. Centre-half Larry Lloyd, nobody's idea of a sensitive soul, was actually one of those and was aware that Clough knew how much he craved his praise. Martin O'Neill was another of the players treading water on Clough's arrival who was transformed but certainly not through undiluted love and affection. In his autobiography, O'Neill recalls being transfixed by Clough's presence the first time his manager walked into the dressing room, and then tells a story relating to half-time in the 1980 European Cup Final, which was O'Neill's first final after injury had ruled him out the year before – something that had hit him hard. On offering to sacrifice himself to a tactical switch that Clough was keen to make, he was stunned to be advised he could stay where he was, so brilliantly was he performing. 'All these years I've searched for his approval, and he waits until half-time in the European Cup Final to give it. I have validation at last. And with those words, energy of which I thought I was bereft jolts through my body like an electric current.'

Clough had played a card he had kept up his sleeve for five years at the perfect moment. He had waited that long to add this balance to what O'Neill referred to as 'every word of splenetic criticism along the way'. Clough once said that it takes less than a minute to change someone's outlook with a word or two and that it was just another form of coaching you don't find in the manuals. Assessing and knowing individuals allied to perfect timing. Such was Clough's aura that his assertion above didn't just apply to his own players. Steve Williams tells of an encounter when he found himself and the Forest manager walking towards each other along a quiet corridor after a match. An admission of trepidation is significant from a character as self-assured as the Saints midfielder, but apprehensive he was as Clough approached: 'You, son, were a credit today,' was all that was said. 'He didn't have to say it,' says Williams, 'but it made a massive difference to me.'

It was a balancing act at which all three excelled – man-management that would be much sought after today in the highest levels of business. Indeed, after his career in the game McMenemy was sought after as a trainer of business managers in motivational skills. Nick Holmes felt McMenemy could enter any walk of life and motivate people, and John Wark highlights the importance of this skill, saying of Robson, 'He knew when to support you and he knew when to have a go at you – and he could do both, always at the right time.' Steve Moran talked similarly of McMenemy, saying he would sometimes have a go and sometimes put an arm around the shoulder. For all the authoritarianism, this was their method of dealing with younger players – a very effective carrot and a much-feared stick. Getting the balance right meant they could get players to run through brick walls for them and strive for a word of praise while never becoming comfortable. It was the perfect combination.

McMenemy's stated wariness of becoming too close to players is interesting considering the undoubted mutual affection between him and his emotional and passionate captain Alan Ball. It's hard to find an example of Clough having an affectionate relationship with one of his players to match the fraternal one shared by McMenemy and Ball – McGovern being perhaps the closest, but that was still seen by both as purely a professional relationship. A player might develop an affection for Clough based first on fear and then respect, but it didn't come the other way. Clearly Clough had a high regard for McGovern, making him captain of many of his teams but, asked if he really *knew* him, McGovern answered, 'I haven't got a clue. He was a believer that familiarity breeds contempt and so he was always wary of close relationships – which was a good thing. He was my boss.' No wonder Clough saw the straight-talking midfielder as an extension of his management on the pitch.

It was Robson who engendered something closest to what might be termed 'love' over a period of time. His belief in the value of loyalty was something that made him special in the eyes of his players and to which many of them owed their success. Arnold Mühren remembers: 'Robson was a real motivator, and so incredibly kind. It was difficult for him to get angry.' Kindness is a word that sticks to Robson, whoever you talk to. It was something he was still demonstrating years later at Barcelona with the young Ronaldo (the first one). His assistant at the time, Jose Mourinho, said, 'This was the best Ronaldo – I never saw the same,' and he put that down to Robson being willing and able to understand the personality rather than just the player. To this day Ronaldo considers Robson a father figure rather than a manager: 'He made me feel so calm, so relaxed – enjoy yourself, have fun.'

It was an approach that would later work for Robson with another mercurial talent who also cherishes him to this day – Paul Gascoigne. 'Talk about father figure,' says Gascoigne, 'the guy was phenomenal for me. Under him I always knew I was safe.' In turn, Robson felt Gazza had to be loved and cherished and treated differently. It fostered both on-pitch genius and a lifelong mutual affection. Gary Lineker recalls the 1986 World Cup tournament, which changed his life, and how easy it would have been for his manager to have listened to the calls to replace him after a run of matches without a goal: 'Bobby made my career what it was. For some reason he stuck with me and I'm eternally grateful for that. I have no doubt that without the influence of Bobby Robson I wouldn't have had the life I've had.'

This empathetic side, the willingness to be, as in the title of Gabriel Clarke's documentary on Robson, *More Than a Manager*, was a part of the management make-up that meant he and McMenemy would be seen by some, particularly those who came through their youth systems, to have brought them up as youngsters away from home. From John Wark at Ipswich to Steve Moran and Danny Wallace at Southampton, many players refer to being coached in life as much as in football. John Wark speaks with genuine fondness and gratitude: 'I lost my father at an early age and Bobby Robson became a father figure to me, not just a manager.' Team-mate George Burley left Scotland at 15 to join Ipswich: 'Bobby Robson brought me up as a person, not just as a player.'

McMenemy too inspired his share of lifelong gratitude from players. Moran also used the term father figure in relation to his manager. As with Wark, Lineker and Gascoigne with Robson, David Peach gives similar credit to McMenemy for support that impacted his whole life, rather than just his career at Southampton: 'He stuck by me for ten years and I owe most of my life to him.' Steve Williams is a straightforward character not short of confidence or an opinion, for which he rightly doesn't apologise: 'You try sharing a dressing room with Mick Channon, Ossie, McCalliog, Jimmy Steele, and see how far you get if you can't stand up for yourself. Too many players don't make it through lack of character.' Even he, however, has no problem acknowledging his affection for his manager and doesn't feel father figure is an overly sentimental term:

> If you had any sort of a problem – football or otherwise – you could knock on his door and know you were going to be invited to put the kettle on and chat. I came

from a tough and poor background. He took a council house kid and showed trust in him. He genuinely cared. As an apprentice I was once told prior to a game, 'Don't turn up if you're not wearing a suit.' I took them at their word. I couldn't afford a suit, so I didn't turn up. Jim McGrath asked where the hell I was, and I told him I was home in Romford and explained why. The next week a suit was delivered to my house. That was Lawrie. Then, also as an apprentice, we were billeted in a terrible guest house. To be fair I'm not sure the club – certainly not Lawrie – knew *how* terrible. Cockroaches and spiders and the like and the kitchen always closed. We were so hungry we stole some apples and were caught. When we explained the background to the story the manager was shocked. Within a week I was moved to digs I loved so much I stayed there for six years. He looked out for you.

Tony Woodcock recalls reading a Matt Busby book in which Busby revealed that one of his favourite letters was from the father of a young apprentice who had been released and which said, 'Unfortunately my lad didn't make it as a footballer, but I'd like to thank you for making him a gentleman.' There was an element of this in each of 'the Three Wise Men' as well as 'the Three Kings'.

McMenemy and Robson's players also talk of good listening skills – another staple of modern management training – although I couldn't find many Forest players who recalled that of Clough. 'He was a good listener,' says Channon of McMenemy. 'He took something from each player who passed through his hands, young and old.' Bryan Hamilton says Robson was similar: 'Bobby had good listening skills. He might not admit you were right, but you'd suddenly realise he'd acted upon it.' After just four months at Portman Road, Arnold Mühren had also made up his mind: 'He is open to new ideas, and you don't get to see that everywhere. Robson is simply an outstanding manager.'

The gift of confidence was a significant consequence of the management style. Many players use the word *trust* frequently in their consideration of why they were such effective leaders of both strong characters and less confident youngsters alike. Clough's captain, John McGovern, says, 'Once he thought you could play, he simply trusted you to go out and do so, he'd expect you to stand on your own two feet and deliver the necessary and it was made clear he trusted you to do so. That breeds confidence.' Tony Woodcock agrees: 'Once he's picked you and you're out there he trusts you to get on with it.' Clough credits this approach to an experience with his own manager at Middlesbrough, Ron Dennison, whose less than reassuring words as he left the dressing room on his debut sent him out on a downer. He felt this was the wrong approach and it was a mistake he was determined never to make in 28 years as a manager. For all his reputation he believed that when footballers go out on to a pitch they must be relaxed, not frightened.

This 'trust breeds confidence' principle also had benefits in fast-tracking the development of talented young players. At Ipswich, Russell Osman was clear:

> We had to go the extra mile – or miles – to get the right young players and Bobby knew that so he invested in Ron Gray and his team and travelled a long way himself. But once you were there, if Bobby felt you were good enough, he'd pick you. I had about 150 first-team appearances by the time I was 23. I remember as well, in the 81 season when injuries kicked in, we had to bring in some less experienced guys. Kevin Steggles had played most of the season in the Football Combination but suddenly had to come in cold for games against Saint-Étienne and Cologne in the UEFA Cup. The last

thing I heard Bobby say to him before the first game was 'I believe in you. You deserve to be playing. You're here for a reason – because you can do the job. We all believe in you – just go out and do it.' And Kevin did. You'd run through a brick wall for him after that.

John Wark also talks of the value of trust, based on his own experience:

> My first-team debut was something else. I'm in the youth team in 75 and suddenly I get a call to go to Filbert Street where I might be needed for an FA Cup replay. And he threw me in, in a quarter-final against Leeds of all people – league champions and about to get to the European Cup Final – up against the likes of Bremner, Giles and Yorath in midfield. It gave me massive belief that he was willing to trust me in a game like that.

McMenemy was, on occasion, willing to trust his youngsters in the most challenging of environments as well, although the suspicion as ever was that at least a small part of doing so was the inevitable media interest it would generate. Such was the case when he put Danny Wallace in to make his debut at Old Trafford in 1980 at the age of 16, the two of them ending up standing together conducting a post-match interview on national television. But regardless, he was demonstrating his trust in a young player on the biggest stage.

Of course, man-management isn't an exact science, dealing as one must with all varieties of individual over the course of long careers, and there were occasions on which McMenemy and Robson felt they got it wrong so dramatically, in emotional circumstances, that both offered to resign. McMenemy's was a confrontation with his young centre-half Mark Wright – another who was not one to take a backward step and perhaps a clash waiting to happen. When Wright threw a disrespectful remark at his manager on the way out for the second half of a match after a confrontational half-time in the dressing room, the two ended up wrestling on the floor in the bathroom. Although McMenemy was clear that, as with Terry Paine ten years before, if his leadership was challenged he had to act, he didn't consider it his finest hour. It reminded him 'how easy it is in an emotional business to go over the top when you should not'. But Steve Williams, who had his own moments with his manager when they didn't see eye to eye, has no issue with it: 'It's passion. If you spend ten years at a club as a player and don't have confrontations, something's wrong. Same for a manager. I want to see passion and if that's how it displays itself sometimes, that's as it should be.'

Robson's physical altercation with Baxter and Carroll years before may have seemed out of character. In fact, his emotional side was never far from the surface all his life and he snapped in that moment and was similarly ashamed of his loss of control. But these were isolated incidents that in their aftermath also demonstrated another element of their shrewd man-management – an ability to then calm troubled waters if it was in their interests.

Peter Rodrigues saw this in McMenemy: 'You knew the line with Lawrie, but he was generally calm and quiet. He rarely lost his rag.' He also points out that this was made easier by clever tactical use of seconds-in-command: 'You need opposites at the top and the next man down.' McMenemy would use Jim Clunie in the sergeant-major role, as would Robson with Cyril Lea, and, to an extent, Clough with Taylor and Ron Fenton. Asked about the coach versus man-manager assessment, Wark recalls, 'Bobby left a lot of the coaching work to Cyril Lea and Bobby Ferguson, though he did set the direction. He gave his coaches licence to be hard on us … and they were!' This sensibly allowed the men in charge to stand one removed from the more standard dressing-downs and retain an air of detachment – making their interventions, when necessary, that much more effective.

It wouldn't be hyperbole, therefore, to suggest that each warranted Mike Brearley's degree in people. There was indeed a genius for man-management in each that was often effectively coaching by another name. The nuances in how they improved individuals, as people as well as players, the way in which they engendered a concrete togetherness and moved players to run through those walls for them and ultimately inspired a lifelong respect and affection, were individual to each of them.

Clough insisted that fear was the last thing he wanted to create, believing nobody can perform at their best hampered by such an emotion. Being a bit wary was perhaps more the aim. It could be, therefore, that the element of fear is somewhat overplayed in analysis of his management but, then again, some of his players may take a different view. Those who, from the outside, saw Clough as arrogant and impossible and would wonder how on earth he earned such respect from those he managed simply have to be referred to his players. Even those whose careers under Clough were accompanied by a mix of apprehension and trepidation saw that they were in the presence of someone special. There was a reason he could rule this way and still be revered by his charges. John Robertson would say, 'He's the most charismatic man I've ever met in my life.' And anyway, in the words of Elizabeth Barrett Browning, 'Since when was genius found respectable?'

1979/80

Southampton
8th First Division
First Division top scorer – Phil Boyer
McMenemy signs Kevin Keegan

Nottingham Forest
5th First Division
League Cup runners-up
FA Cup round 5
EUROPEAN CUP WINNERS

Ipswich Town
3rd First Division
FA Cup quarter-final
UEFA Cup round 2

The Potter's Heron Hotel near Lawrie McMenemy's home in the genteel suburb of Romsey has never seen a gathering like it. The press men and television cameras fill the large but now cramped room McMenemy has chosen for his greatest conjuring trick. He's wondering how he's managed to keep the secret over the last few weeks and is looking forward to putting the subterfuge behind him at last. It's Monday, 11 February 1980 – an unremarkable day by any standards and the ever-sceptical media corps mutter to each other about what they're doing here. They're not going to be best pleased at being dragged to the shires if McMenemy is about to offer them an injury update. What's he up to?

With the love of the dramatic gesture that sustained his ego, the manager strings things out with a few minutes of idle chat. Then he asks his chairman to open the connecting door behind him and says, after a pause for further dramatic effect, 'Gentlemen, this is why you are here,' and he invites the throng to behold 'a man who is going to play a big part in the future of this football club'. Into the room walks two-time European Footballer of the Year Kevin Keegan – one of the most feted and recognised players in the world. A stunned silence not normally associated with hard-bitten press men is broken by another uncharacteristic act – a spontaneous and sustained round of applause. Little Southampton, and Big Lawrie, have just pulled off one of the most astonishing coups in the history of football transfers and in this moment they've become a club to be reckoned with and known all around the world.

The story of 1979/80 is one of three moments, one at each club. Although finally relinquishing their three-year hold on the League Cup after another final appearance, and finishing in the top six once again, Forest's season was once more all about the European Cup. If winning it had surprised the whole of Europe, retaining it meant it had to sit up and take serious notice. Forest could now lay claim to being the most dominant team on the continent. Another away win against all predictions and logic, this time in Berlin, made real Clough's belief that they could go anywhere and beat anybody. He wouldn't have known it was to be his last silverware for nine years, but for now he could bask in the profile of being pre-eminent across Europe.

Ipswich continued to build towards their *annus mirabilis* of the following season, with Frans Thijssen having joined his compatriot Arnold Mühren early in 1979 to complete a midfield that, along with John Wark, was to become the most effective in Europe. For several of the players, the moment they realised just how good they might become came on the first day of March when they took Manchester United to the cleaners to the tune of 6-0. It produced no trophy in itself but was another of those special moments that live forever in the memories of the supporters. It wasn't just the players for whom that match stands out as a moment in time. Eight years old at the time, Tim Smith still remembers the impression it made on him: 'That was the moment of realisation, 6-0 against United. That was when I felt it could really happen – that my little team were at the top table. Thinking of it again today reminds me it wasn't just the trophies – it was definitely about special days and results like that.'

After the consolidation of the previous season, Southampton were beginning to give notice that they would become one of the most entertaining, free-scoring and dangerous teams of the next few years. Only Liverpool and Ipswich (narrowly) exceeded Saints' 65 goals, and striker Phil Boyer was to benefit from the style of play to finish as the division's top goalscorer. Adding to the supporters' anticipation of watching a team of entertainers, McMenemy brought back the prodigal son Channon. But all was to pale into significance alongside the moment that put Southampton into the top strata of national and international consciousness and media focus – and it didn't happen on the pitch.

You're the One for Me

*'He had this knack of attracting the best players
in the country to come and play for a small
provincial club.'*

Nick Holmes on McMenemy

The signing by Southampton of Kevin Keegan, in a successfully clandestine manner most would have considered impossible, was a jaw-dropping moment that would lead directly to the title challenges of the next two seasons. Above all, it was indicative of the cunning, persistence and personality that McMenemy used to recruit players everyone else would have considered beyond him. It was one thing in which it could be argued he outperformed even Robson and Clough; it certainly showed a slightly different approach to the building of teams and finding the sort of player who would make the difference.

Keegan's team-mate David Armstrong felt, 'For me Kevin and Lawrie changed the whole outlook of the club, and it has remained a high-profile club ever since. Without Lawrie that wouldn't have happened.' As McMenemy pointed out, little Southampton had trumped far bigger and wealthier clubs and he knew this would enhance the name of Southampton across Europe. It filled fans like me with an enormous sense of pride, and David Dykes clearly saw the significance too: 'That signing was huge because it was the first time Saints had competed at that level.'

It was McMenemy's personality, ambition, belief and selling skills that had led them to this altitude. It also demonstrated his ever-increasing love of creating a bit of theatre as his own profile continued to grow. He would refer to this as his signature policy and certainly it was a huge part of the McMenemy persona. Peter Osgood recalled, of his own decision to join Saints, which also surprised the football world: 'He said he had a five-year plan and was going to build a side around me. Considering he had Mick Channon and Terry Paine, I thought that was fantastic.' But it wasn't just the big-name signings on whom this persona was influential. Left-back David Peach was one of McMenemy's first and shrewdest signings. On his decision to join him from Gillingham, Peach says, 'He was a big giant when I met him and I thought, *What have we got here?* You look up to him – he's big in stature and has got a big personality.'

The three managers knew their personal impact could seal these unexpected deals, aided by a bit of tactical although genuine empathy. If there were special targets, they would make sure they met with the player, and often his wife and family just as importantly, reassuring them that the club, and they personally, would find them the right house and generally smooth the transition to their new home. Robson and McMenemy in particular made a point of ensuring their new signings were looked after in every detail. They would take an interest in how they were settling in at home. Arnold Mühren's wife Gerrie recalled how much they both valued the way Robson made them feel at home, and Kevin Beattie, often prone to a degree of homesickness, also refers to his manager making him feel comfortable straight away.

This extra care wasn't something offered for purely tactical purposes. It undoubtedly helped get the best out of players, but it came from their own set of values. They also had an ability to sell not just the club but the place and community. McMenemy would use the tranquillity of the New Forest as a draw – somewhere where they could make a home, find good schools, and neither they nor their families would be bothered by people as they would undoubtedly be in the big cities. This was just another example of the mutual benefit that arose from the close relationships between these clubs and their communities and the managers' acknowledgement and inherent understanding of the value of them.

The Keegan signing was, according to the player himself, due to McMenemy's 'big, charismatic personality, his talent for man-motivation and his infectious enthusiasm'. He could just as easily have been talking of Clough or Robson, although the idea of Clough and Keegan in the same dressing room boggles the mind. One of Clough's most important signings in completing his trophy-winning squad was Archie Gemmill, who was apparently perfectly settled and happy at Derby County where he had won two First Division titles in seven years but who had little hesitation in moving to Forest for one reason only: 'He didn't have to sell Forest to me – it was *him*.' And if, as many believe, Allan Hunter was indeed Robson's key signing and greatest influence on the path to success, he too chose Ipswich due to the individual he saw before him: 'There were a lot of offers for me, but I joined Ipswich after meeting Bobby Robson. Within five minutes I had no doubt Ipswich was the place I wanted to go.'

Once they identified a player they were determined to capture, this power of personality was employed to swing the deals ahead of often more illustrious rivals. And capture was the right word. There are plenty of examples of each, having decided 'you're the one for me', holding players as good as hostage until pen was put to paper. It may raise a smile now, but it could not, and did not, fail to make a significant impression on those they were detaining under lock and key. They may have been man-managers, but they were also consummate salesmen. The clinching argument would often be convincing and then proving to these players that they would help them prolong their careers when others considered them past their best. In return they got commitment and performances from players that others considered unreliable luxuries. That ability to get the best out of players who might otherwise not have achieved all that they could was part of the overall tool set.

McMenemy insisted it was his policy to buy the best, even if others thought their peak years had been and gone. For all the Keegans and Shiltons that were to come, McMenemy considered his most critical signing that of Osgood in 1974 because it was the first of the statement acquisitions. The manager referred to him as his pathfinder. Eyebrows were raised when the King of Stamford Bridge and the King's Road agreed to come to the south coast, but it bought McMenemy credibility at a difficult moment. The manager understood that Osgood's presence would not only make for a stronger team but would offer notice to the game nationally that they should sit up and take notice. It confirmed the ambition of Southampton FC. His own programme notes for the first home match after Osgood had signed began by flagging his gratitude to his directors for backing him all the way in spending more money than the club had ever done before, but then also highlighted some of the reasons he had gone for him, other than pure footballing ability. These included an ability to lift the other players around him and to put a few thousand on the gate, the latter being something to which McMenemy was always wise and evidenced that he was ever conscious of the need to promote the club and increase its limited revenue potential.

Such signings, to him, had greater potential benefits at a club like Southampton than could be measured purely in the goals-scored column. Osgood gives the credit to those McMenemy selling skills. He wrote in his autobiography, 'Lawrie McMenemy is a persuasive man, as I was to find out when he welcomed me at the door of his house and then shut the door behind him. I was surprised to see him locking it, saying, "You are not leaving this house until you sign for Southampton.'"

Similarly, Clough would never let a player think about it over the weekend, and when he wanted that player he would stick to him like glue and let nobody else get a sniff. Robson used the tactic in the pursuit of one of the two Dutchmen he had identified as the players to take his 81 team to the very top, Arnold Mühren. It must have meant something to Mühren to find the manager sitting in his kitchen in Volendam, inviting him to join him on the next flight to Ipswich and giving the distinct impression that he wouldn't be leaving his house until he had agreed to do just that. On 17 August 1978 Mühren not only signed for Ipswich but became the first-ever full-time Dutch professional to play in England.

There were distinctions between the three when it came to the critical signings. As suggested, McMenemy was fond of the grand unveiling and the star name that would make headlines, and this was more important to him than it was to Clough and Robson. After the championship success, Clough did move in this direction with the signing of Trevor Francis as the first million-pound English player and the media circus that went with it. It was, however, perhaps not his forte in comparison with McMenemy, and his subsequent attempts to repeat the trick with a string of expensive buys over the next few years were disastrous.

Robson, by contrast, was happy to go under the radar and took satisfaction in pulling off his transfer coups at a financial level that kept his club on an even keel. Bob Harris saw him balancing the books as if the money was his own, 'helping him to fund the next crop of bargains'. On the same day that the £1m Francis deal was announced, Robson signed Frans Thijssen for £200,000 – a player who would become Footballer of the Year within two seasons. Robson had now secured two high-class Dutch internationals for a combined cost one third of that Clough had paid for Francis.

McMenemy too was capable of finding a gem at little cost. This is where the confidence to manage players with a reputation that scared off others, justified or otherwise, opened the door to bargains. Steve Williams played with two high-class left-backs in his time at Southampton and Arsenal, 'But while Arsenal paid a million quid for Kenny Sansom, Lawrie took Mark Dennis for free. And although if you wanted an international, Kenny was probably ahead, if you were after consistently the best performances over a First Division season, Mark was the man.'

Clough was less interested in following the fashion for recruiting foreign players after the 1978 World Cup when a combination of Argentina's victory and *Evita* in the West End seemed to send the country and its football managers into a frenzy over South Americans and others besides. While McMenemy went for Ivan Golac and Robson brought in Thijssen and Mühren to complete his finest team, Clough was less trusting, saying, with impressive self-awareness, 'Foreigners have difficulty in understanding me and I sure enough cannot understand them.' As befitted his rather 'Little Englander' character, Clough preferred to stick to what he knew, although whether any of those players could understand him and his methods either is by no means a given. Interestingly, when Thijssen signed for Clough three years after he had for Ipswich, he didn't enjoy anything like the same success and was gone within a few months, which suggests Clough's self-analysis was right all along. Thijssen confirms the issue: 'It went wrong in the first conversation I had with Brian Clough, and we simply didn't click. He may have been a good man-manager but for me it didn't work.' After years in the care of the more genial Robson, perhaps it was never going to.

The importance of securing Alan Ball for McMenemy has already been explained; the method by which he managed to bring such a player to Southampton has not. On meeting

Ball in his office, McMenemy promptly locked the door à la his Osgood tactic, advising him he wouldn't unlock it until he had signed. It may have appeared a joke, but it gave Ball the assurance that this manager valued him more than any other. And it worked. Ball became McMenemy's leader and voice both on and off the pitch, and in identifying those players who would make a key difference, this idea of a trusted lieutenant with the experience and respect to carry out the role was often significant. Where McMenemy had Ball, Clough had complete trust in John McGovern and, at Ipswich, Robson's lieutenant and on-pitch leader was Mick Mills. None of them the most expensive signings, but every one a jewel in their manager's eyes. Clough based the evolution of his team from dirt-trackers to European champions on the ability to regularly unearth those diamonds who made a huge difference to the whole. In fact, that ability should more accurately be credited to Peter Taylor, who McGovern refers to as 'the ultimate recruitment officer'. Woodcock agrees: 'It was about knowing, really understanding, what qualities a player has got and assessing character. This is where Peter Taylor was important rather than on the training pitch – he could judge a player in seconds and see small things that would make a big difference.'

Peter Rodrigues, brought in on that free transfer in the summer of 1975, had a particular reason for being grateful for the power of the McMenemy sales pitch: 'I played at Southampton with Wednesday in the 74/75 season and I remember Lawrie being booed from dressing room to dugout. I said to myself that I would never, ever sign for that club. By that July I was in his first-team squad!' And by the following May he was accepting the FA Cup from Her Majesty The Queen.

1980/81

Southampton
6th First Division
FA Cup round 5
Lawrie McMenemy turns down Manchester United

Nottingham Forest
7th First Division
FA Cup quarter-final
European Cup round 1

Ipswich Town
Runners-up First Division
FA Cup semi-final
UEFA CUP WINNERS
European Team of the Year
Football Writers' Player of the Year – Frans Thijssen
PFA Player of the Year – John Wark

An FA Cup semi-final from another era at a packed Villa Park. A corner is swung in from the left and met by an unmarked Kevin Beattie who powers his header towards the bottom corner. The oldest man on the pitch, Tommy Hutchison, somehow scrambles it off the line. Next, a free kick and Beattie again, this header so powerful it flies over the bar. Second half and another corner, Beattie first to it for the third time. Six yards out and determined to keep his header down to hit the target, the ball hits the rock-hard ground and bounces up and over the bar in an act that appears to defy the angles of mathematics. Still the most likely match-winner and the team's talisman, Beattie goes into a tackle and comes out with a broken arm – his season over in an instant. Ipswich's treble chance is over just an hour later …

… three weeks to the day, the last day of most people's season but not that of Ipswich, whose cup-tie exploits require them to play four more times – at Middlesbrough today and the last league match, which should win them the title if Villa lose today, and two legs of the UEFA Cup Final, the first just four days from now. Ipswich are ahead at Ayresome Park and comfortable at half-time; Villa are going down at Arsenal; the season's efforts are about to be rewarded. Big Bosco Janković is an unlikely kingmaker but twice in a row he heads into the Ipswich net. ITV's commentator confirms, 'Ipswich's title hopes right down the drain' …

… four days on, Robson's team are asked to find the strength of body and of character to try to win the UEFA Cup. Paul Mariner completes a 3-0 home leg win. A fortnight later, as Mühren's corner is flicked on by Mariner, John Wark's 14th goal of the campaign equals the record for a European competition. More than that, it settles the tie and wins Ipswich their first-ever European trophy. From the ashes of the season's bitter end they've secured their place in history.

Southampton's newfound profile, their season of undiluted excitement and entertainment – the 4-4 draw at Tottenham on Boxing Day being typical – with McMenemy having turned down Manchester United and now bestriding the English game, had the manager and everyone else believing they had every bit as much chance of winning the First Division as United themselves, and McMenemy cited Ipswich as the inspiration. For Ipswich were to be the story of 1980/81.

A seventh-place finish and an FA Cup quarter-final hardly suggested Forest falling off a cliff but their dominance was gone and, for a year or two, Clough would acknowledge he and Taylor took their eyes off the ball, became a little complacent and diverted away from the methods that had produced the success with a succession of expensive and surprising signings, none of whom was to make a success of it. The names of Justin Fashanu, who perplexed and irritated Clough beyond belief before he handed him on to McMenemy within 18 months, Ian Wallace and Peter Ward, who all arrived within a year from July 1980 for a then preposterous combined £3m, may still initiate a little shudder in Forest fans of the time.

But for Ipswich this was to be the year – one of huge achievement and desperate heartbreak. For most of the season looking likely and worthy winners of an unprecedented treble, injuries within a limited squad had them losing crucial matches at the season's end. Although the UEFA Cup, their first-ever European success, wasn't insignificant compensation, to this day the season has become one tinged with regret at the 'what might have beens'. It particularly sticks in the craw of many of the players that Ipswich beat the Aston Villa team that pipped them to the title three times that season – home, away and FA Cup. Their insistence that this proved their superiority is hard to dispute. The loss of four of their last five league fixtures was the issue. Even then, Villa lost their last match when needing a point for the title and Ipswich could have taken that title by winning at Middlesbrough. They lost the match and, with it, the opportunity. In the FA Cup, by the time they met Manchester City in the semi-final they were clear favourites to win it. It was a day when the fates seemed to be against them, and an extra-time free kick saw them beaten.

The UEFA Cup became their salvation. It wasn't just the winning of the trophy, but the way they did it, thrashing many respected European teams home and away and creating more of those moments that meant so much to their followers. Such was their dominance it's worth a brief recap: Ipswich 5 Aris Salonika 1; Ipswich 3 Bohemians Prague 0; Ipswich 5

Widzew Łódź 0; Saint-Étienne 1 Ipswich 4; crack German team Cologne beaten home and away in the semi-final and, in the final first leg, Ipswich 3 AZ Alkmaar 0. In total, 28 goals in 11 matches – an indication of their style of play and their belief. The definitive performance – the magic moment – was going to Saint-Étienne, past European Cup finalists liberally sprinkled with major internationals, and humiliating them on their own ground.

The sense of lasting pride Robson felt when his players achieved an unprecedented 1-2-3 in the voting for the PFA Player of the Year in the persons of John Wark, Frans Thijssen and Paul Mariner was only topped when Ipswich – little, provincial Ipswich – were named European Team of the Year. An astonishing achievement completely far-fetched in the days when he was suffering the chants of 'Robson out'. The players are very clear about the one thing that mattered above all others, and that's echoed by Saints and Forest players of the time about their own success – togetherness.

Coaching or man-management? Tony Woodcock gets the Souness treatment during Forest's 2-0 first round, first leg European Cup win. Woodcock would supply both of the goals which knocked out the holders from an unaccustomed position on the right, thanks to the subtle intervention of his manager

Spinning straw into gold. John Robertson's goal wins the 1980 European Cup. Clough's genius turned the self-confessed slob into the most effective winger in Europe

His greatest conjuring trick. McMenemy reveals Kevin Keegan to a stunned press corps at The Potters Heron Hotel in Romsey, February 1980 and puts Southampton on the global football map

Clough and his team celebrate an FA Cup win at Spurs in his first match in charge. The creation of a togetherness which would move mountains is the reason for their success most frequently referenced by players of all three clubs

The ability to evolve sides to attain specific goals was vital to sustained success. In 1984 McMenemy achieved a new defensive parsimony built on Peter Shilton and Mark Wright, whilst retaining a key player who connected them to the 1981/82 team, Steve Williams

So near and yet … Ipswich's assault on the treble starts to unravel in April 1981 as Kevin Beattie is lost to a broken arm in the FA Cup semi-final

'It was terrible. I never felt so bad after a game.' Nick Holmes (left of picture), the only constant in all McMenemy's teams, on this FA Cup semi-final defeat which ended their double hopes. Adrian Heath's winner in the last minute of extra time was the first goal they had conceded in the entire competition.

Forest's defeat by Anderlecht in the 1984 UEFA Cup semi-final was later confirmed to have been overseen by a corrupt referee, Guruceta Muro (extreme right). Clough was never to manage in European competition again.

The end of the road. One got the timing of his departure right, one felt later that he left when there was more still to achieve, and one stayed too long – a source of lasting regret to himself and his admirers. Here a pensive McMenemy seems to be questioning his own timing as he leaves Southampton for the last time on the way to his unsuccessful tenure at Sunderland

Legacy … the time of our lives. The homecomings and the bond between managers, players, and communities can never be erased. These places came alive as never before or since. This was their greatest gift

Legacy … lessons for the ages.
The game's most decorated current
manager, Pep Guardiola, says
his success and particularly his
management of players, is based on
what he learnt under Robson

A banner at St Mary's in 2006 indicative of the belief of many that the soul of the club and the McMenemy legacy has been casually discarded

Too good to be forgotten ...

Together We Are Beautiful

*'The capacity and the will to rally men to a
common purpose, and the character which
inspires confidence.'*

Field Marshal Montgomery (on his definition
of leadership)

The Australian fast bowler Glenn McGrath once reflected on what it was that made the team he graced for a decade one of the most successful cricket teams of all time:

> The thing I think I enjoyed most was that we became a very close unit. I spoke to a few of my team-mates about what made us successful, and they said they felt it was because we really cared about each other, and I think that's important. We enjoyed each other's success as much as our own, and if you've got a team or a unit, whether in sport or in the workplace, where you can really gel like that then you're definitely on a winner.

The word *togetherness* was a constant when asking the players of the three clubs whether they could pinpoint the key to their successes and why it still means so much to so many of them today. The managers set out specifically to create this and it became a natural by-product of all their other actions. They cultivated it as far as possible without it becoming a hostage to fortune when tough decisions had to be made. There's no mention of the sort of cliques one often hears of today. One big happy family might seem a rather twee description of what existed at the three clubs but the players' testimonies suggest it's the truth and the managers absolutely understood its importance. In Archie Gemmill's words, 'That's what winning teams are all about.' Clough once said, 'Show me a club that has laughter in its dressing room as well as talent in its team and I'll show you a club that will win things.' It was another simple philosophy that served them all well and allowed them to bear out Clough's words.

What exactly determined this *esprit de corps*? It was partly simple mateship – that they enjoyed each other's company and would socialise together as well as play together, and it's not insignificant that many still do so to this day. It was also again a matter of trust. They would look around the dressing room and see no bad apples – you could rely on the guy next to you to go through a brick wall for you and have your back in any situation. And it was based on having fun. After all, as Channon said, football was just his hobby. They were having the most unexpected time of their lives. Coming from nothing, with little expectation from those outside that they were about to change the face of the game, not only reduced any negativity brought on by pressure to succeed but meant that the 'us against the world' mentality was easily bred.

Drinking together may not be something from the modern-day Arsène Wenger school of dressing-room culture but it formed an important part of the bonding experience, and McMenemy, Clough and Robson were all wise to its benefits – on occasions positively encouraging it as part of both team bonding and the release of pressure – perhaps the most famous example being that insistence of Clough that his players should share the table of champagne prior to the 1979 League Cup Final. (Those of us with a nostalgic fondness for 1970s football – not to mention champagne – and all that came with it, miss such tales, and can't help feeling the game is the lesser for their disappearance.) The level of togetherness is something John McGovern for one is sure couldn't be replicated today.

Above all, perhaps, it was a lack of the ego and jealousies inherent in the make-up of many a modern player, but not one that suggests the cast was lacking characters. Woodcock considers this critical: 'I look at that Forest side and there was a character in just about every position, but nobody was above anyone else.' Hughie Fisher also has little doubt where the success came from at Southampton: 'The single most important factor in us winning the cup was togetherness. We were a team – no animosity and no cliques. We were all mates which was our great strength.' At Ipswich this was fostered by the fact that so many of the 1981 team grew up together. John Wark remembers, 'We all came through the youth team together, so we were real mates – and we still are.'

The supporters could appreciate this too. Tim Smith says of Robson, 'He just built something where the players had that belief – in him and in each other; that collectively they were more than the sum of their parts.' Robson summed it up when considering the success of his players: 'On the pitch they had a real work ethic, but then off the pitch they had fun. They were pals and that was important.'

It gave them the edge over teams studded with more high-profile individuals and instilled a willingness to do the hard yards for others rather than letting the next guy do it, which allowed them to sustain the success even once the element of surprise had gone. The managers weren't slow to use the perceived scepticism of the critics of the potential for success and the ambitions at these smaller clubs to foster the siege mentality and increase the determination to prove people wrong. Forest's Ian Bowyer felt 'it was a bit like us against the media because we felt we were seen as a provincial club, and we didn't quite get the rewards or credit that our football or results deserved'. And there's a hint of McMenemy's dig at Jimmy Hill about the media's ambivalence after the 1976 FA Cup win in Steve Williams's recollection of Mick Channon suggesting to him that if he went to Arsenal in 1980, he would win 50 England caps; if he stayed where he was, he would probably get none. He was making the point that England managers didn't come to The Dell, 'which I thought was a disgrace'. These were bugbears of longstanding for the managers and, as ever, it was something they turned to their advantage.

The fact that club finances dictated limited squad sizes may have ultimately cost them trophies, but it had a benefit too in cementing this togetherness. Tim Smith makes the point that 'all three teams, you could name their starting XI. In fact, I probably still can. That must have bred consistency and spirit.' Like Tim, to this day I can run off the names in those regular starting line-ups – not just that of my own team but the other two as well, which may say something about me, but also reinforces the point that the teams truly *were* teams.

Back to McMenemy's comments on what his time in the Guards taught him that was to have a direct bearing on his management approach: he believed that a squad of players was no different to a squad of guardsmen and that you must know your men, accept them as individuals and make them into a team, which neatly captures the essence of what he, Clough and Robson were able to create like few others before them.

1981/82

Southampton
7th First Division
UEFA Cup round 2
First Division top scorer – Kevin Keegan
PFA Player of the Year – Kevin Keegan
PFA Young Player of the Year – Steve Moran

Nottingham Forest
12th First Division
League Cup quarter-final

Ipswich Town
Runners-up First Division
FA Cup round 5
League Cup semi-final
UEFA Cup round 1
Bobby Robson leaves at the end of the season

Middlesbrough away, at Ayresome Park, on a dark and cold late January day. It's not the first choice of many players as the match to look forward to and get excited about when scanning the season's fixture list. But today it's one to set the hearts racing at Southampton. Eight minutes in, Kevin Keegan rounds Jim Platt and puts Southampton ahead. In an act of justice, the softest of second-half penalties for Middlesbrough is blazed wide by Bobby Thomson. Otherwise, Saints are barely in trouble and see out the victory. Before five o'clock the news comes through that

Manchester United have lost at Swansea. Southampton
Football Club are top of the First Division for the first time
in their history, looking down on 91 other clubs. Lawrie
*McMenemy has literally reached the pinn*acle.

If 1980/81 could be seen as a missed opportunity for Ipswich, 1981/82 was to prove the same, but this time for Southampton as well. And for one club, one manager and one iconic player, its conclusion marked the end of the road.

Nottingham Forest's waning powers in the wake of the bizarre recent transfer policy and the departure of some of the key experienced players from the European Cup-winning teams produced a bottom-half finish in the league and not a great deal else. For Ipswich and Southampton, however, the season saw them still close to their very best.

Robson's men couldn't replicate the charge on all fronts of the previous season and probably hadn't the physical or emotional energy left to do so, which makes their runners-up finish to the inevitable Liverpool all the more praiseworthy. This was, Robson knew in his heart, his last chance to land the ultimate prize. Again they were agonisingly close; again they suffered crucial injuries in the run-in – not least the broken shin that ended Thijssen's season. It was Brian Clough and Nottingham Forest who consigned them to second again, with a 3-1 win at Portman Road. They were still capable of bursts of dominance, winning nine in a row in all competitions over Christmas and six from seven towards the season's end. It was never quite enough to suggest they would catch Liverpool but a top-six finish for the ninth of ten consecutive seasons showed a consistency for a club of their relatively limited resources unmatched before or since.

Southampton suffered another sobering experience in Europe, the arena they never managed to conquer, with a 4-2 home defeat by Sporting Lisbon, whose fast passing game ruthlessly exposed Saints' vulnerability in defence. That weakness was ultimately to cost them a potential league title – one that McMenemy never felt was out of their reach until he left the club. The team of Keegan, Channon, Charlie George, Dave Watson and Alan Ball was finally clicking and at The Dell they were almost untouchable. A run of 11 wins and only two defeats in 17 matches around the turn of the year included another red-letter day for the club. On 30 January that Keegan goal took them to the top of the First Division, for the first and only time. McMenemy had achieved one ambition – all he had to do now was maintain it.

Unfortunately, the 18th match in that sequence was a 5-2 loss at the hands of Ipswich – specifically at the hands of the five-goal Alan Brazil – and after several happy weeks leading the race they were off the top. The hammering was an experience from which they never recovered, losing seven of their last 13 matches to finish in a deflating sixth place, which was no accurate reflection of their impact upon the season. Like Ipswich the previous year they were partly undone by the inherent and insoluble disadvantage of the smaller club – a lack of squad strength when the injuries kicked in. Crucial this time was the loss of Steve Moran, and with him his goals and his partnership with Keegan, to a back injury at the end of March. Moran's strike partner was a man for whom this conclusion was particularly anticlimactic. Keegan felt winning the title with a club like Southampton would be one of his most impressive achievements. His success had also been built on a phenomenal drive and ambition and a hatred of losing. On the coach journey back from Middlesbrough, Keegan had stressed to McMenemy that he felt with one more significant signing, Peter Shilton being the man he had in mind, the holy grail would now be achieved. McMenemy demurred, partly because he couldn't see his mate Clough selling Shilton. It sowed the seed in Keegan's mind that the club did not, after all, match his ambition and it takes its place in that list of sliding-doors moments. Shilton duly arrived that summer, just weeks after Keegan departed, the irony and frustration of which never left the fans thereafter.

If it's arguable whether McMenemy had made the wrong call over that additional signing, there's not much doubt that, for once, two months later, he briefly lost his genius for man-management after the 3-0 home defeat to Aston Villa that confirmed that the title had gone. Accusing Keegan of not trying, even indirectly as a challenge to the whole team, was misjudged and was to cost him his star player, and with him went his best opportunity to achieve his ultimate goal. A furious Keegan, his anger fuelled by both episodes, insisted he would leave at the end of the season and leave McMenemy's broken jigsaw behind him for the manager to survey. The club kept the imminent departure as quiet as possible, much to the indignation of those fans who then bought season tickets expecting to see Keegan lead the next tilt at the title. He, along with his young protégé and partner up front Moran, had swept the board at the PFA Awards. He was a man and player it was going to be difficult to replace.

In the story of *Too Good to Be Forgotten*, the other departure at the season's end was even more significant. After ignoring all the big-club blandishments over the years, a patriot of Robson's commitment wasn't able to turn down the call of his country. It would bring down the curtain on a period of the club's history never to be repeated. Robson was to go on to further success; Ipswich were not.

McMenemy, by contrast, stayed on. What the Keegan departure, and what he saw as the deficiencies that cost him the title, told him was that the jigsaw he had so carefully worked on, and so nearly completed, needed to be put away and a new one started. If team building was one skill he shared with Robson and Clough, another was knowing when to evolve it, however painful it may be to rip it up and start again.

Rip it Up and Start Again

'Taylor and I were always at our best and fired
with the greatest enthusiasm when we were
dismantling teams and rebuilding them, rather
than maintaining standards already set.'

Brian Clough

The most remarkable feature of what was achieved at these clubs was longevity, which is what, for me, places the achievements above that of the Leicester City miracle, as one example. Clough often said that it was harder to maintain success than achieve it – words that were both sincere and somewhat ironic given, of the three, his period of greatest success was considerably shorter, if more intense. Perhaps this was a consequence of his own character – certainly at both Derby and Forest the success shone spectacularly but burned out more quickly. His less volcanic and mercurial contemporaries spread their glory days over a greater distance; they generally aimed to change one or two players a season as an evolution – Clough later admitted that his revolution approach in the early 80s was a mistake that curtailed his success and blamed it on changing approach, worrying about age rather than talent, as a result of becoming arrogant and considering without pause that every call he and Taylor made was right.

Robson, McMenemy and, for a time, Clough all appeared to have a sixth sense for the moment to make adjustments, which was an indication of their inner drive to always go one better rather than to rest on what others would see as laudable achievements. Robson was clear he had to evolve to maintain and improve upon existing success and, consequently, he built three distinct teams: 'I had a good team in 1975, a trophy-winning side in 1978, but my best was the class of '81.' And for all the flamboyance and star men of the 1980–1982 Southampton teams, Steve Williams nominates that of 1984, underpinned by Mark Wright and Peter Shilton, as the finest, or certainly most effective, in which he played.

When it came to making the changes, concerned supporters had to learn to trust their manager's judgement. Looking back, Tim Smith is clear how his team was evolved: 'There was a lot of change between 1978 and 1981 – you had two different teams. Everyone today thinks of it as a continuum, but in fact they were very different.' Smith's fellow fan Terry Hunt wrote, 'Robson's management was masterful. He continually refreshed and strengthened the team. For example, the arrival of Mühren and Thijssen took Town to a new level.'

As a young Southampton fan, the eventual but inevitable departure of Mick Channon to a First Division club the year after the FA Cup win felt like a disaster and perhaps the end of our ambitions; in fact, within a year Saints were promoted and within three Channon was very happy to return to The Dell. Likewise, Clough's acceding to the sale of Tony Woodcock after the first European Cup win raised eyebrows but less so when another European Cup arrived the following year. Robson's sale of Brian Talbot straight after an FA Cup Final win in which he had been instrumental may have seemed brave or foolhardy depending on your opinion but, before long, at a fraction of the price he achieved for Talbot, in came Thijssen and the team improved further. Many Ipswich fans would have been aghast at the sale of David Johnson to Liverpool in the summer of 1976 – a vital character and player in the 1975 team who scored 35 goals in 136 appearances – but Paul Mariner arrived to replace him and ended up with 260 appearances, 96 goals, domestic and

European honours and the status of an Ipswich legend. Having already acknowledged the importance of Hunter and Beattie as centre-halves on which the 75 and 78 teams were built, the gradual, almost imperceptible, transfer from this partnership to that of Terry Butcher and Russell Osman led to even greater success. And it's no coincidence that those players had been integrated over time under the wing of their predecessors, learning as they went. No element of talent and experience was wasted with an eye to the longer-term picture.

It was all evolution carefully calculated to produce teams tailored to specific objectives. 'The clever bit was that he realised that he had the players who could win a cup but not win a 42-game marathon, so he changed approach.' So says Steve Williams of the 1976/77 and 1977/78 Southampton teams in which he was a common presence. McMenemy knew full well that his FA Cup winners weren't the ones to get him out of the Second Division (indeed that XI never played another match together after Wembley) and it was a revised and more pragmatic team that achieved the promotion goal two years later. Then the big names started to be reintegrated once established in the top flight and with ambitions to win the biggest prize. McMenemy felt that the money in the bank he had with the supporters might decrease if he couldn't get them back to the top division soon. He evolved the squad to that end, bolstering it and making it fit for a dogfight. The team that achieved promotion two years on from the cup win contained only four survivors from Wembley. Once there, he was already planning the one or two additions that would be needed to stay there as he tweaked the team again.

That balance that McMenemy sought between the closeness to his players that would encourage commitment and the distance required to make pragmatic decisions regardless of individual relationships was a prerequisite in this drive for constant improvement. Another of those values learned early in life underpinned this. Honesty. That, in turn, sustains respect.

Clough understood that players won't work for managers they don't respect. Honesty was an important part of gaining that respect, however tough it might be on an individual. A player needs to know where he stands and to hear difficult truths if respect and trust are to exist. They were willing to make tough calls and be prepared to explain them. Ian Bowyer said of Clough that 'he was just straight with people and expected you to be straight back'. Classic Clough in this regard was the case of Peter Withe, the striker whose goals had helped Forest to the title and who believed, therefore, that he should and would be a part of the resultant European Cup campaign the following season. 'He was wrong, that's all,' said Clough, who felt the money on offer and the timing was right to move him on and that was the end of the matter. In came the local boy Garry Birtles, who helped secure two trophies and scored 25 goals in the process – 11 more than Withe the previous season. Job done.

Saints' centre-half Paul Bennett played his part in the cup success, not least in helping the team to negotiate with aplomb a difficult away quarter-final. At the end of that season, however, McMenemy advised him that he was being released. Bennett recalls it hit him hard and led to a departure that wasn't on the best of terms, but he tells a story of meeting McMenemy years later at a public event where his erstwhile manager admitted to him that he may have got this one wrong and let him go too soon. Whatever frustration that may have engendered in his former player was now offset by a respect for McMenemy's honesty and the relationship was happily repaired.

An understanding of the need to work within their own more limited budgets wasn't foreign to three men whose upbringings had taught them the value of managing money. Robson said it was a matter of personal pride for him not just to play good football at Ipswich but to keep them in the black. He always tried to spend the club's money as if it were his own – pure Langley Park and not a philosophy dear to the hearts of Premier League managers today. Bryan Hamilton nods to Robson's canny proficiency in this area: 'The team always evolved, he brought me in and sold me, he started to play Roger Osborne, he bought Johnson and sold him and brought in Mariner. There was steady, continuous progress. Bobby did it brilliantly. Gentle evolution was the way he had to do it, because he didn't have the big cheque book.'

It was when Clough lost his way in this facet of his management in the early 80s that things started to unravel at Forest and it's fair to note that his attempts to regenerate were by no means as successful, or at least that they took longer to bear any fruit, which may have something to do with the idiosyncrasies of his behaviour, the disregard for a tactical plan and the creation of a togetherness within a tight group that wasn't easy to penetrate. A ballplayer of Frans Thijssen's ability ought to have been the perfect fit but it didn't come off, and the big-money moves for the likes of Ward, Fashanu and Wallace looked more like desperation than evolution, bringing in characters not quite in tune with the group. The foreign players Clough did eventually go for in this period were forgettable. Raimondo Ponte and Einar Aas made just 42 appearances between them before Clough made good his prediction that he and the overseas player wouldn't be a comfortable combination, and today they're the preserve of the football statistician alone. In truth, in the case of Clough's Forest it appeared that if you were a part of the initial evolution it worked, but coming in from the outside having not been part of the growth process was much harder. For whatever reason, the rebuilding of teams as opposed to their initial construction was one of the few areas in which Clough would have to concede he wasn't quite as astute as his two rivals, his words at the start of this chapter therefore open to scrutiny. The tweaking of what he had, yes, but more significant reconstruction, perhaps not.

1982/83

Southampton
12th First Division
UEFA Cup round 1

Nottingham Forest
5th First Division
League Cup quarter-final

Ipswich Town
9th First Division
FA Cup round 5
UEFA Cup round 1

Two weeks in September 1982.
Saturday, 18 September. Ipswich are playing their third home match of the post–Robson era. They have one point from the previous two. They're hosting a Stoke City team that for the last decade they would have expected to put away. They've fought back from two down early on and are heading for a disappointing home draw. But in injury time Stoke striker Paul Maguire scores to consign them to a second home defeat. That night's table shows Ipswich Town bottom of the First Division. In 11 days' time they'll beat AS Roma in the first round of the UEFA Cup but not by enough to prevent elimination after a heavy defeat in Rome. They won't play in Europe again for another 19 years.
Saturday, 25 September. The atmosphere of anticlimax after the departure of Kevin Keegan still hangs heavy over

Southampton. Neither supporters nor players appear to be able to snap themselves out of it. They've already lost 4-1 at home to newly promoted Watford and 6-0 at Tottenham; the team is suddenly unrecognisable from the feared, all-out attacking, title-chasing model of the previous two years. Now they're heading to Anfield to take on the champions. By five o'clock they're leaving on the wrong end of a 5-0 scoreline. They've just taken over from Ipswich at the bottom of the First Division. Peter Shilton has arrived as the intended final piece of the jigsaw. He's conceded 18 goals in his first seven matches. Four days later a 0-0 draw in Sweden sees them knocked out of Europe at the first hurdle by the part-timers of Norrköping. Something is missing.

Saturday, 25 September. Nottingham Forest travel to Tottenham. They've suffered reverses of 3-0 to Manchester United, 4-3 to Liverpool and 4-1 to Aston Villa within their first six matches. Today they go down 4-1. They've conceded 16 goals in their first seven matches. The Forest team contains just two of the players who won the European Cup a little over two years before. Nobody seems quite sure how it has happened. On this Saturday night, Ipswich, Southampton and Nottingham Forest have played 21 league matches between them this season. They've managed a combined total of five victories.

The season of 1982/83 was to be the lull, with clubs, managers and fans alike trying to deal with the anticlimax of the Keegan, Robson and Peter Taylor departures, and in Forest's case the loss of one of their own statement players, Trevor Francis, and the rock on which 1978–1980 was built, Kenny Burns. The early part of the season was to suggest none of the three had adapted well. It was a lull from which McMenemy, and eventually Clough, would rescue their clubs to differing degrees. For Ipswich it was a post-Robson vortex from which they would never escape.

In attempting to replace Keegan, the loan signing of Fashanu and the permanent acquisition of Keith Cassells from Oxford United were rather like hoping that Joe Dolce could act as an acceptable stand-in for Frank Sinatra. The rumour was, however, that Cassells had in fact been a makeweight in negotiations for McMenemy to secure a talented if unknown centre-half. Mark Wright was to be the cornerstone of the change in playing style and to become an England World Cup player. He was another McMenemy masterstroke. However, it was going to take time to assimilate the new players, and in the meantime the heavy defeats of the early season seemed to come match on match. McMenemy's frustrations in Europe also reached a peak in this down period, with the elimination at the hands of Norrköping vying for worst experience of the lot. A recovery of sorts was affected but it would be another 12 months before the new team would prove McMenemy still had it.

Forest's unremarkable season was further evidence that their best days were behind them. That said, an improved league position of fifth marked something of an upturn and meant they were back in Europe. Clough, too, would demonstrate in the next 12 months that his powers hadn't yet completely deserted him, building a young team that played football that was very easy on the eye, while behaving like choirboys under his strict parental guidance. Clough took justifiable pride in what he had built through a group of young players, memorably suggesting his only issue with the squad at that time wasn't injuries but acne.

While Southampton and Forest had the men in place to help them bounce back, Ipswich no longer had such good fortune. An immediate and ongoing decline merely reinforced what Robson had meant to the club. Ninth this season would be followed by 12th and then 17th as the team Bobby built began to break up and its players sensed it was over and took their leave.

Thanks, but No Thanks

'I felt if the new stadium went ahead, there was tremendous scope for us all. I looked around, I was surrounded by friendly, intelligent faces who were swaying me their way.'

Lawrie McMenemy
(on turning down Sunderland – the first time)

If the gradual adaptation of teams was one factor in the ongoing nature of their success, the other was, rather obviously, the fact that they remained in situ, resisting temptations to move, for a length of time that would be highly unlikely at such clubs today. To achieve a long period of success, first the clubs had to retain their managers in the face of inevitable interest from others. It was nigh-on unthinkable that a manager delivering these sorts of results would turn down the likes of Manchester United, and all that came with them, as both McMenemy and Robson did, to remain at provincial clubs. (In fact, for a while at Southampton McMenemy was English football's longest-serving manager.) Their success brought with it any number of suitors and should they have proven irresistible this book would have been significantly shorter. When the likes of Manchester United, Leeds and Sunderland came calling, why would managers with genuine ambition decide to turn them away?

The reasons stretched from loyalty, to power, belief and contentment. The first was common to McMenemy and

Robson and there's no doubt that this is where that loyalty shown to them by their employers in the past came to the clubs' rescue. Even though Southampton's directors weren't *too* gentlemanly to openly put that card on the table in front of McMenemy when they had to, mutual loyalty, not something widespread in the game or business of today, was the glue through which the relationships endured and the glory days evolved. Even then it might be disingenuous to suggest that this on its own was the determining factor. Both were, at different times – sometimes at the same time – extremely torn.

They were also aware that the 'my way' control they had established over their clubs wouldn't be so easily replicated higher up the chain. That hegemony, and the autonomy to run the clubs from top to bottom as they saw fit, were things they valued significantly. They had no desire to be intolerably shackled as they would have been at the biggest clubs – their characters and their methods wouldn't wear it. It may be true that if any managers might have been able to run the show at such major clubs, these three would have been the most likely to make it work, and Alex Ferguson ultimately proved it could be done by the right personality, but this was still the exception that proved the rule.

Thirdly, they didn't get to the summit without huge self-belief, and they all felt they could still achieve their highest ambitions at these clubs and the satisfaction of doing so would rank for them as a greater and more rewarding achievement. They didn't believe at the time that they had realised the full potential of what they had built and in which they had invested so much. There was still unfinished business. Even when McMenemy eventually left for Sunderland in 1985 he would later reflect that he perhaps left slightly too soon and that a title at Southampton might still have been attainable. Ipswich's players of the early 80s, while understanding he couldn't turn down his country, felt that when Robson left in 1982 there was still more to achieve. Russell Osman remains convinced they could have stayed together as a team for another couple of years at least.

When McMenemy was conflicted over the United approach from Sir Matt Busby, Ted Bates asked him what he thought he could achieve at Old Trafford that he couldn't at Southampton. The fact that the manager saw this as a very fair question perhaps says more about where he had taken the club than anything else, articulating how he had indeed broken the football mould. Sir Matt and Martin Edwards may have taken issue with Bates's leading question, but they were not to get their man. They weren't to land Robson either, for precisely the same reasons. McMenemy had weighed up the satisfaction he had in his job and his view that his club was already better on the pitch than many of those pursuing his services and still had the potential to progress, and he came down on the side of staying put, as he had two years previously in saying a polite 'no thanks' to Leeds and Sunderland (first time around). In his memoir he stops short of saying that rejecting the chance to manage Manchester United was a mistake but neither did he deny regular post-retirement reflections on what might have been. Ironically, when he did eventually leave, some of those factors behind previous decisions to remain were still in play and this time any regrets were more about what he might have achieved had he stayed.

Similarly, Robson recalled an offer from Everton in 1977, which he had effectively accepted before a change of heart. In his rapprochement with his chairman, he was clear about how torn he was between his loyalty and his ambition, but ultimately knew where his heart lay, saying how Everton was a 'bigger club' and that he was ambitious but that Ipswich had been good to him when he was a nobody, and ever since, and that he loved it there. He may have later wondered about the wisdom of not taking the new challenge but each time one such came along both he and McMenemy came to the same conclusion.

Finally, the increasing contentment all three enjoyed from living in attractive places – with the settled, happy lives enjoyed by their families of particular importance to them – and being around good people at their clubs and in their communities, wasn't to be forsaken without serious consideration. Put simply, they were happy.

Had the managers left when given the chance there's little doubt that many players would have followed them out of the door, as happened at Southampton and Ipswich when that time did eventually come, another indication that it was the managers themselves for whom the players were playing as much as the clubs, and that the whole adventure was intrinsically linked to them as individuals.

1983/84

Southampton
Runners-up First Division
FA Cup semi-final

Nottingham Forest
3rd First Division
UEFA Cup semi-final

Ipswich Town
12th First Division

16 March 1984.
Southampton sit fifth in the First Division, 11 points
adrift of the leaders – Liverpool, naturally – but with two
matches in hand. Liverpool will win a treble within two
months but, tonight at a Dell buzzing with electricity,
McMenemy's men know that a victory against the team
from Anfield will put them in serious contention. The title
ambition that most assumed had left with Kevin Keegan
is now very real once more. Mark Dennis runs on to a pass
on the left, his deep cross is headed back across the penalty
area by Frank Worthington, McMenemy's 'rascal' for the
season, but it's behind Danny Wallace and the chance has
faded away ... until Wallace launches himself horizontally
and smashes an overhead kick into the roof of the net – the
goal of season contest ending here and now. He adds another.
It's not the 2-0 win that makes the statement about how

far the 'little club' has come and its newfound status as a major football force, or even the relative ease with which it has been achieved against a team often cited as that great club's finest of all. It's the fact that it's not a surprise. Nobody wants to play Southampton anymore – not even European champions-in-waiting. The gap at the top is closing, the anticipation of what may be to come is building. Four days later Saints thrash Sheffield Wednesday 5-1 to reach the FA Cup semi-final and talk of a double is no longer greeted with mirth. History and McMenemy's ultimate ambition are in sight …

… another classic 1980s FA Cup semi-final Saturday, the quality of the match, as so often, denuded by the size of the prize on offer, and an atmosphere of tension but huge noise and colour in the stands. Highbury is as iconic and traditional a semi-final venue as the Villa Park setting for Ipswich three years before. The favourites Southampton are challenging at the top of the league and are here as a result of away wins in every round without a single goal conceded, McMenemy's team's reputation for defensive generosity now well and truly buried. Their luck in the draw hasn't improved as, in Birmingham, Watford are doing battle with Third Division Plymouth, while Saints have to face an increasingly confident Everton emerging under Howard Kendall. In fact, Everton are just 12 months away from the title and a European trophy. It's a dog of a match with not an inch between the teams; Southampton are struggling to get the pace of Moran and Wallace into the match, while Williams and Armstrong versus Reid and Bracewell is a midfield arm wrestle with no obvious winner. It's not in Saints' favour that their captain and greatest influence, Williams, isn't fully fit – injected up to the nines for a brave but ultimately inevitably below-par performance. For two hours there's no sign of a goal either. Into extra time, then to the very last minute of 120; Reuben Agboola has the

chance to clear the ball down by his own corner flag but dallies and fouls Peter Reid. Reid's free kick is deflected on and Saints hesitate. The ball bounces up in front of Adrian Heath and the smallest man on the pitch heads it in. After nine and a half hours of FA Cup football Southampton concede their first goal. It as good as ends their season, and their possible double, without a second available to respond. In an atmosphere of month-long anticlimax, Southampton will still finish runners-up in the First Division – bested only by the greatest Liverpool team in living memory. It's the highest finish in Saints' history. Neither they nor their manager will ever walk this way again.

The season of 1983/84 would offer evidence that McMenemy knew how to rebuild teams and that Clough had rediscovered the habit, and both would come close to major honours again. It would also reconfirm for Ipswich that life without Robson would see no such resurrection.

For all the pizazz and star quality of McMenemy's 80–82 teams, many fans would agree that his best team, certainly in terms of efficiency and consistency, was the one that found itself in the chase for an unlikely double. With Moran still scoring goals and now supplemented by the pace and skill of a young Danny Wallace, and a central midfield pairing to match any other in Williams and Armstrong, they still offered danger in attack. The difference, however, was a defence at last worthy of the name built around Mark Wright, and a new sweeper system that allowed attacking full-backs Ivan Golac and Mark Dennis (the last of McMenemy's semi-tamed rascals) to bomb forward. The new miserly model worked so well that Saints achieved their highest-ever finish as runners-up – another piece of club history on McMenemy's CV.

In reality, they were always some way behind Liverpool. In the FA Cup, however, they soon became firm favourites.

To lose a semi-final they had been expected to win in the final minute of extra time to the first goal they had conceded in just shy of ten hours of cup football was galling and was put on the increasing pile of 'what ifs'. The only survivor from the 76 final playing that day was Nick Holmes, a local lad whose time at the club bookended the McMenemy years and who was the only constant in all the teams the manager built. This match was the most devasting of his career: 'It was such an unjust outcome, but it was their year. It was terrible. I've never felt so bad after a game.'

For Clough, back to something like his best post-Taylor with third place in the league, the same unjust fate awaited his young team in Europe. Not for the first time in his career he was touched by a raging sense of injustice over a European tie. He was convinced the referee for the UEFA Cup semi-final with Anderlecht had been 'got at'. At the time it seemed like just another well-worn Clough response to defeat on the continent; in due course he was shown to have been 100 per cent correct, with bribery proven. This corroboration did little over the years to assuage his anger that his chance of a last European trophy had been taken from him by foul means.

There were no such stories of near misses and injustices for Ipswich. Only their second bottom-half finish since 1972 was accompanied by little else of note. Their die appeared to be cast.

1984/85

Southampton
5th First Division
FA Cup round 5
UEFA Cup round 1
Lawrie McMenemy leaves at end of season

Nottingham Forest
9th First Division
UEFA Cup round 1

Ipswich Town
17th First Division
FA Cup quarter-final
League Cup semi-final

Heysel tragedy – English clubs banned from
European football.

*Southampton arrive at the City Ground, Nottingham
on a February afternoon in 1985. There's no sense of
portentous history in the air. Of all the battles between the
two managers and their clubs over the previous decade,
including cup ties, titanic encounters at the top end of the
Second and then First Divisions, and one classic Wembley
final, this one feels unremarkable. It plays out as such with
a 2-0 Forest win. Neither team could suggest they were
a serious part of the title race; neither would be in any
trouble at the other end either. Encounters between the two*

had never, in ten years, suggested anything close to going through the motions. This one is coming close. It is in fact an appropriate metaphor for something more significant than just both teams' seasons drawing to a close. Nobody knows it today but, when the final whistle blows, a curtain is coming down. The three managers are destined never to be in direct competition again.

We arrive at our end point. At the finale of 1984/85 McMenemy would finally leave for Sunderland. His parting gift had been fifth place and, in theory, another European campaign the following season.

In the cups, Ipswich rolled back the years with a quarter-final and semi-final, but 17th place meant that from here on their battles would be at the other end of the table to that to which they had become happily accustomed.

And at Forest the promise of the previous year wasn't borne out by ninth place and a first-round departure from Europe. There was to be no more Europe for a while – for anyone. On 29 May 1985 at the Heysel Stadium a tragedy, the responsibility for which was laid primarily at the door of English supporters, took that away for the foreseeable future. McMenemy, Clough and Robson would never manage these clubs in Europe again, and given the role it had played in the story of the three wise men it seems the most appropriate place for the story to stop. We have reached the end of the road.

The End of the Road

*'I had a beautiful job, with beautiful people, and
I gave it all up to try to win the World Cup.'*

Sir Bobby Robson

All good things, of course ...

The breakup of a special relationship, perhaps even more
so when that relationship came as an unexpected surprise
in the first place, leaves a void. If you sense that it was so
special that it's unlikely to come round again, the emptiness
lingers. Change may be inevitable but accepting it when it
brings to an end something that has brought great pleasure
is an unwelcome task. The hope is that the personnel might
change but the story remain the same. It's usually a vain hope
and so it was here.

When Michael Parkinson left his BBC Radio 2 *Sunday
Supplement* show (a gentle mixture of paper reviews, interviews
the likes of which only Parky could secure and conduct, and the
'Great American Songbook'), which had become something
of a treasured institution over 11 years, he was inundated with
messages pleading with him not to go. Instead, the last letter
he read on his final show was the one he claimed struck the
right note: 'Go if you must, but please leave us the music.' He
was insistent he had picked the right time to go.

In the case of Robson, McMenemy and Clough, their
respective decisions as to when they should depart can,
with hindsight, be seen as ranging from the judicious to
the regrettable, and unfortunately for the players, the fans

219

and the places to whom they had given so much, the music itself was to fade, gradually but significantly once they were gone.

Robson had of course exited first, with Ipswich at the peak of their powers and he at the height of his reputation, to take on the England manager's job. In due course the respect for Robson abroad would reach another level, culminating in his being voted European Manager of the Year in 1997. He was, perhaps, always the most likely to go on and on … his boundless energy was never going to be satisfied with inactivity. That said, biographer Bob Harris rightly brings things back to Suffolk: 'For all of Bobby's success with England, Newcastle, PSV, Porto, and Sporting Lisbon his greatest legacy is with Ipswich Town.' McMenemy also took his leave at the top of his game, with Southampton having finished second and fifth in his last two seasons, although his disastrous two seasons at Sunderland prefaced something of a petering out of momentum and an underwhelming finish to a remarkable career. Clough, as is well documented, was the one who assuredly stayed too long, missing any number of opportunities to ride off into the sunset on a high.

Tim Smith recounted to me his own witnessing of the end of an era at Ipswich:

> There was Bobby, and then with Bobby Ferguson, who took over, we were trying to convince ourselves and hang on to the Robson era, as Ferguson had been his right-hand man. But when Bobby left and then the Cobbolds moved on, the whole thing changed. Robson was undoubtedly the best thing to happen to Ipswich – the town as well as the club.

The hangover from Robson's departure and the sense things would never be the same again took immediate effect, with Ipswich bottom of the table six matches into the next season.

There was a recovery of sorts, but it was dawning on most that significant decline was now only a matter of time. John Wark, for one, felt it. I asked whether Robson leaving was a significant factor in his own decision to depart for Liverpool: 'Yes, all day long. Players started to go after Bobby left, with money suddenly becoming a factor in a way it hadn't been while he was there, and I just thought, *I can't see us winning things anymore.*'

By March 1983, Mills, Mühren, Thijssen and Brazil had followed Wark out of the club, each departure feeling to the fans like a light going out. Tim Smith offers a further fan's perspective on the end of the era:

> In 86 we played Sheffield Wednesday away and lost and were relegated, and Terry Butcher announced he was leaving and that, for me, finally closed the door on that era at the club. But, of course, it was an almost inevitable consequence of the loss of Bobby to England, which therefore I guess was the beginning of the end.

McMenemy could never shake the feeling that he could have stayed and still achieved more at Southampton, and that was endorsed by another top-six finish and, but for Heysel, a place in Europe the following season. There had been no discernible decline and perhaps there could indeed have been more successes. He would later say that he should probably have taken a six-month sabbatical and returned refreshed to move forward towards the ultimate goal: 'I should not have done what I did, that's for sure.' The reality was that McMenemy had enjoyed his place in the sun and was not to find the same climate anywhere else in the future. My memory, however, will always recall him foremost in these years.

Clough had come through the fallow period from 1981 to 1983 and had now rebuilt a youthful and attractive team ready to push for honours again, if not at the level of the glory days.

A driving force for Clough after the acrimonious split from Taylor in 1982 was the need to prove he could do it alone, amid murmurings that he couldn't, in the immediate aftermath of the breakup of that relationship. The proof point for this was supposed to be the 1984 UEFA Cup in which Forest reached the semi-final and would have reached the final but for that corrupt refereeing performance. Missing the last chance of another European trophy, along with the FA Cup Final defeat seven years later, perhaps meant he found it tougher to let go before the ultimate decline took over.

He still felt he could deliver silverware. There was a lot to admire in the years that followed and flickering reminders of the magic of the man through his youthful, enthusiastic team. Clough may have been glossing his legacy slightly by suggesting that the building of another team that would win two League Cups was, in the circumstances in which the club found itself, as impressive as his First Division title, but he was clearly proud and pleased to prove himself once again. But it wasn't quite the same and never would be or could be.

It feels appropriate that Clough's final season should be the first of the new Premier League (his Forest actually hosting the new competition's very first live Sky match), given it was this vehicle that would begin the journey to a place where the methods and the achievements of a Clough and a Forest can never be repeated. The Premier League and its attendant trappings would have been anathema to him in just about every way, and as a signpost that it was time to wave a final, fond goodbye to all that these managers had given us, it was the perfect creation. In the words of Bryan Hamilton, 'The whole role of the manager and preparation has changed, starting with the likes of Arsène Wenger in the 90s. You wouldn't be allowed to manage like they did anymore.'

Legacy

Precious Memories,
Timeless Lessons

The Oxford English Dictionary defines legacy, in the sense in which we're using it here, as 'the long-lasting impact of particular events, actions, etc. that took place in the past, or of a person's life'. The legacies of the three wise men can be broken into two. The first is the gift of nostalgic memories for communities that had never experienced such success and happiness before and haven't since; the second is the blueprint for management and leadership that many striving for success today in sport and other spheres would do well to study. There's nothing new under the sun. They gave their communities the time of their lives, and their achievements and methods hold a value too good to be forgotten.

The Time of Our Lives

'Saints became as-near-as-dammit as close to
a glamour team as a small-town club could
ever hope to get.'

Peter Batt, Mick Channon biographer

'I have quoted it many times, but I also
believed the football club was an integral part
of the community.'

Lawrie McMenemy

'They're still my team and everybody knows it.'

John Wark

'It will never happen again in terms of the
connection between the players and clubs and the
community. These days you're lucky if you have
three players from the same country in the team if
you're trying to win the Champions League. We
had more than three players from the same town.'

Tony Woodcock

'If I was with another football club back then I
wouldn't have wanted to go to The Dell on a
Tuesday night, or a dark Saturday afternoon
knowing this lot are going to go right at you and
if they go one-up it'll be three before you know it.'

Steve Williams

*'Lawrie and what he did will always be special,
because he did it FIRST.'*

David Dykes, Southampton fan 66 years and counting …

*'It was a hell of a homecoming. The landlord
of a little pub was dumbstruck when we
rolled in for refreshments. Everyone in the
whole area was enraptured.'*

Bobby Robson (on returning to
Ipswich with the FA Cup)

*'Ipswich was growing as a town back then
but there's no doubt the supporters embraced
the team and that made a difference – the
two were very close.'*

Bryan Hamilton

*'It was a great club, a confident club, from the
chairman down. We believed we could do things other
people said we couldn't because in their eyes we were
"Ipswich Town … a small club". And we ended up the
best team in Europe. We did it. Special days.'*

Allan Hunter

*'I think the city grew up with the team.
Those homecomings were when I realised
what this means to the people.'*

Larry Lloyd, Nottingham Forest

*'It was that decade that put Ipswich
Town Football Club, and Ipswich the
town, on the map.'*

Russell Osman

*'Southampton will always be a little club
compared to Manchester United but from the
moment we won the Cup we became a big little
club, admired by a worldwide audience for our
audacity and our will to win against the odds
with a very high skill level.'*

Lawrie McMenemy

*'The Southampton team was like a Who's Who of star
players in the 1980s and that was down to Lawrie.'*

Nick Holmes

*'Ipswich was a very sheltered place when
I was growing up. Nothing else was going
to put it on the map.'*

Tim Smith, lifelong Ipswich fan

*'We played in the right way, expressing
ourselves and sending those fans home with a
smile on their faces. We did that every single
week at The Dell, which is why everyone
associated with the club has got such fond
memories of this particular era.'*

David Armstrong, Southampton 1981–86

'It was good for the town – you could see it from the town centre, which was buzzing. And the decline of the club over the years has been matched by a decline in the town centre too, which isn't a coincidence – success for the club and the town went hand in hand.'

Russell Osman

'Saints finished seventh in 68/69 and in 70/71, but there was no feeling of potentially winning the league. But by the early 80s under Lawrie, we genuinely started to believe we had a shot.'

David Dykes

'I was just so pleased for the recognition the city would get as a result via the football club. Deep, deep satisfaction and huge pleasure.'

David Dykes on Saints' FA Cup win in 1976

'I didn't think that Southampton had so many people. Everywhere you turned the streets were packed. I never thought that winning the Cup would mean so much to so many people.'

Ian Turner, Southampton goalkeeper 1976, on the FA Cup homecoming

*'What Bobby did was fantastic, 81 and
all that, and 81 was the best side. Bobby's
real skill was in these building blocks and
allowing things to grow, but it was John
Cobbold who gave him the time to do it –
and that won't happen again today.'*

Bryan Hamilton

*'It's that thing of putting your town on the
map that meant the most to me. I grew up
in a relatively sheltered village that was
never going to be big news. Growing up
with the feeling of "this is my town" is hugely
influential on you as a person. I may have
left at 22, but today Ipswich is still home.'*

Tim Smith, Tractor Boy for life

This is why it mattered – the creation of a bond between clubs, players and their communities of a type that will never be seen in quite the same way again. Bobby Robson's words above encapsulate why the success meant so much to so many, and still does. While this is certainly a book about remarkable success, it's really about the wider impact on three places and their people. This relationship wasn't simply a coincidental by-product of the football success – the three managers who made it happen understood its value and encouraged their players to nurture it at every turn. As former Newcastle chairman Sir John Hall said, 'When you live in a mining village, you live in a community, it's never about yourself, it's always about other people.' There's a book on Brian Clough, *The Fans Behind the Legend*, by Steve Brookes, in which the myriad stories of the man's kindness and thoughtfulness when connecting with the people of Nottingham amply demonstrate the store he placed in such things, Brookes contending that his aura will be around the club forever.

Lawrie McMenemy's belief in the relationship with his community, and his understanding of where that connection between hometown and fan came from, mirrored that of his two contemporaries. Sadly, it was to appear less important to some of those in whose care his club would land in the decades to come. Saints' FA Cup winner Jim McCalliog tells a tale of travelling back from the semi-final when he and Peter Osgood were encouraging McMenemy to stop for a drink. The pub was full of Saints fans and McCalliog remembers with affection the mutual happiness and sharing drinks with their fans for a good hour. Different times for sure.

It's not something I can express in a single sentence, but for a slightly left-field reference on this rapport between home and football club, the television celebrity cook and one half of the Hairy Bikers, Si King, whose unlikely inclusion here is justified by his lifelong devotion to his home-city club Newcastle United, and therefore the passion for football in that area that began this story, explained in a TalkSPORT interview why, just as Robson articulates above, he believes a pride in one's home and surroundings is a fundamental element of many football fans' allegiance:

> It's about that six-year-old lad, or lass, stood there at their first football game and going, 'This is me; this is what I am; this is where I am; this is my people; this is where I'm grounded; this is where I feel I belong,' and that's what football fans are about, and that's what it is. It's about that recognition and that attachment to the place that you live and love.

Tim Smith reinforces the sentiment when considering his relationship with Ipswich – the town – through his football team:

You have that affiliation with the town. I grew up in a small village in Suffolk where some of the players lived. I don't think you ever lose that connection. For me a community needs somewhere to go together. I suppose the church was once the ultimate, but our football club in those days is where our community came together. It was a sense of belonging, and when there's success, of course people want to be part of it. That's what Bobby Robson did for Ipswich.

The conflation of church and football ground feels valid. These old stadiums did indeed become places of communal experience and celebration. While it might be stretching it to see Brian Clough, Bobby Robson and Lawrie McMenemy as pastors of their parishes, they did have the characteristics of those able to encourage faith and lead a flock, and each managed to cultivate and cement such attachments through their achievements and their own firm understanding of their wider impact. This is, to my mind, their single greatest contribution. It's their legacy every bit as much as the details in the record books and the remarkable, consistent success they delivered.

While the three clubs were of course rivals for the same prizes and accolades during this time, as a Saints fan I always felt more of a kinship with such clubs than with the established big-city names and was rarely unhappy to see them successful when not in direct competition. My suspicion that there might be some sort of unspoken brotherhood between fans of smaller clubs, whose environments and experiences are shared and understood, was borne out during conversations with followers of each of these teams. There was a degree of affection for them within the game because they were 'nice people' and could be more intimate with those with whom they came into contact than was possible at big clubs.

This was a point Clive Thomas, the referee in Saints' cup final win, made when explaining why he reflects with pleasure on their victory. (This was many years later. I would never suggest that this affection had anything to do with the marginal onside call that accompanied the winning goal.) 'There was a family atmosphere at Southampton – always a cup of tea and a sandwich. I found it to be an extremely friendly club. Not all clubs are like that – some are too big to be friendly.' And the opposing manager that day, Tommy Docherty, reinforces that view: 'If I had to lose to anyone it would've been Southampton Football Club. The people in charge were always very hospitable. Win, lose, or draw they were always the same. They were lovely people.'

It was a part of what made these clubs popular outside their own domains – they put a smile on people's faces and gave others who followed smaller clubs the chance to dream. The pride of the clubs' fans was heightened by this sense that others were enjoying them too. Today the idea of 'everyone's favourite second team' has been rather lost in a sea of envy and a societal demand for one's own instant gratification rather than taking pleasure in the deeds and happiness of others.

Forest fan Richard Collier was slightly too young to experience the full detail of 1977–80, but he does vividly remember the European Cup turning up one day at his local cricket club and carrying it around the field with one of the players. It was just one leg of its tour, being brought to the community to whom it meant so much. Cherished memories of these special days aren't the exclusive preserve of the fans either. Forest's John O'Hare felt that, 'It's amazing how much football means to people's lives. There was a sense of "it's my town, or my city, and I want to be proud of it".' But he suggests the players felt it too when he says, 'I'd like to think all the supporters had the time of their lives as well.'

In researching this book, the thing that struck me most was the enduring comradeship between many of the players and the fact that so many have chosen to make these communities their homes to this day, regardless of background or even, in some cases, nationality. When making arrangements to meet with the four Ipswich players who contributed their thoughts in person, I assumed I would be travelling to London, perhaps even Scotland. The person making the introductions was amused: 'No, just go to Ipswich. All the guys still live within about 15 minutes of each other.' John Wark, for example, a proud Scot who spent successful years with the mighty Liverpool – at the time, the club that would be the pinnacle of most players' ambitions – talks of an unbreakable, almost ethereal connection to the club, the town and its people. He still lives in Suffolk. At Forest, the likes of John Robertson, Frank Clark and Colin Barrett, from Lanarkshire, County Durham and Stockport respectively, still live in the area today. Kevin Beattie highlighted the connection that so many of the players felt for people and place: 'The Suffolk people are so nice – once you're in with them you're there for life. So many ex-players still live around Ipswich because once you're here you don't want to leave.'

Peter Rodrigues played for 15 seasons with three other clubs, making 387 appearances; he was at Southampton for two seasons where he played 59 times. And yet, he states, 'When I finished, that was my club. You knew it was a family club. Everything about it – the players, the manager, the directors, the people.' And in company with every other player from the three clubs, those people – their publics – truly meant something to him, something that was ingrained by the memories of the homecomings in the days following the greatest successes. In Rodrigues's case 'On the bus into the city bringing the cup home, on Shirley High Street, I looked down and saw two old guys in floods of tears and I thought, *Pow! These people have really come out for us, and this is what it means.*' Peter Rodrigues still lives in a suburb of Southampton today.

The social consequence of their successes may have taken a little longer to register with certain players, despite the exhortations of their managers, but the penny dropped in the end. Tony Woodcock feels that 'at the start as a young, ambitious player you're focused on yourself and not saying "how do we come together to do something for the community?" It's only when you start winning things that you see the effect it has.' And what an effect.

Ah, those homecomings. The litany of memories in the words of those involved bring to life the days of people's lives. The Saints players still display incredulity when talking about their welcome from the Southampton public on returning with the FA Cup. David Peach remembered, 'I've never seen anything like it, and I don't think any homecoming side has had a reception like we got.' The moment in time is as treasured a memory for those players as it is for the people. Centre-half Mel Blyth recalls: 'To this day it's the most people who have ever turned out in the city. The elation, you just can't put into words. I could've stayed on that bus all day long.'

It was a true moment of connection between the club and the public. The air that day was sweet. McMenemy tells the story of stopping off at a local factory on the journey back from the cup final. Running late for the official reception in the city centre he was determined to keep a promise. The cup was handed round the shift workers to a mixture of tears and cheers. He reflected, 'That's what local teams willingly do. These are the memories that live with you. We were sharing the most wonderful experience.' Arriving at the Guildhall, via 19 miles of packed streets, to find 200,000 people squashed into the civic centre car parks meant something to manager and players alike: 'This was our community, and they were thanking us in what I've been told was the greatest public show of affection since the end of the Second World War.' David Dykes was, of course, there as a fan: 'I'm Southampton born and bred, and I can remember my first game, Christmas Eve 1955. In 70-odd years I've never seen the city like that.' This reaction to an FA Cup win might produce puzzlement in the young fan of today but not Dykes: 'Winning the FA Cup then really mattered. It was more impactful than the First Division, which is why Bobby Robson and Lawrie McMenemy's bringing home of that trophy was worth more than those who weren't there would understand.'

And the new experiences – Europe, for example, and the unique atmosphere of the matches under floodlights. Previously this seemed the exclusive domain of the Manchester Uniteds and Celtics of the world. These nights were gifts bestowed by the managers and their abilities and took their sleepy communities into the consciousness of people all over the continent.

So, at the end what do we conclude about the days of our lives as Southampton, Ipswich and Forest fans? The trophies that did come were unexpected and truly special – but they alone are not the definitive measure of the 'glory days'. *Saint–Étienne 0 Ipswich 4; Ipswich 6 Manchester United 0; Manchester United 0 Nottingham Forest 4; Southampton 4 Marseille 0; Liverpool 0 Southampton 1; Middlesbrough 0 Southampton 1.*

These are the days, and nights, that remain forever in our hearts and memories. A match illustrating this is one I recall personally, having been present and then watching it back on *The Big Match*. December 1981, Southampton 3 Manchester United 2. Ultimately the win didn't lead to a title, although perhaps it should have done, but for me it remains the encapsulation of those halcyon days – the anticipation in the Friday night queue, hoping for a successful outcome at the ticket office; the Saturday morning excitement of *expecting to win* as we really did in those days, which seems so far-fetched today; a dark pre-Christmas afternoon, floodlights and packed stands; the United of Robson, Moses, Wilkins and Big Ron in town; a Saints team filled with Keegans, Channons and Balls;

the greatest disallowed goal ever scored and a late winner; a rerun on national telly on the Sunday and further justification that little Southampton were a team that could beat the best in the land and win the title.

These are the days that tell the story for me, and for many others – even more so for the feeling that we're playing a different game today – and it's not just the fans of *our* three clubs in this story who should mourn them. As Tim Smith suggests, 'This time was important not just for these three places, but for football itself,' and he also feels it was the spirit of the age that adds to his affection – the idea that these teams achieved such special things while having a ball, perhaps *because* they were having a ball, is one we fans can associate with and we thank the managers for their semi-indulgence of it. Smith remembers of Ipswich, 'The manager would turn a blind eye to an extent to the drinking culture, but made the players realise they had to perform on the pitch. In the end the fact that they managed to do both at the same time just endears us to those days even more because I suspect it is the way any fan would like to do it themselves.'

The era was extra-special because of who we were. These achievements were not those of a Liverpool or a United and somehow that meant more. Kevin Keegan alludes to this from a player's point of view in his own autobiography *My Life in Football*:

> I surprised myself about how much I liked the idea [of signing for Southampton]. While there was something exciting about playing in front of huge crowds at Liverpool and Hamburg, I could imagine that the satisfaction of leading an unfashionable, unheralded team to their first-ever league title might far outweigh that of doing it at a club where it was almost second nature.

It didn't happen. Not quite. But, as I say, in a sense it doesn't matter. These days were about experiences we had never tasted before; about two cities and one town finally *being something*; about the sense of pride and belonging that came with being put on the map and being, for once, in the national and international consciousness; about being allowed to dream and expecting to win; about being the ones who broke the mould.

Lawrie, Brian, Bobby, thank you for those Elysian days – for the time of our lives.

Epilogue

Too Good to Be Forgotten

Ill fares the land, to hastening ill a prey,
Where wealth accumulates and men decay ...

... but times are altered; trade's unfeeling train
Usurp the land and dispossess the swain;
Along the lawn, where scattered hamlets rose,
Unwieldly wealth and cumbrous pomp repose ...

... Those healthful sports that graced the peaceful scene,
Lived in each look and brightened all the green;
These, far departing, seek a kinder shore,
And rural mirth and manners are no more.

Oliver Goldsmith, excerpts from 'The Deserted Village'

Our game is changed, and so is our relationship with it, particularly for those of us who follow clubs such as these. The poet's suggestion above, that invasive wealth was responsible for the change in character and ultimate decay of the village of Auburn, may seem counter-intuitive if money is deemed to be the most obvious facilitator of prosperity; the counter being that it often also encourages greed and materialism at the expense of something fundamentally more precious.

Auburn may or may not have had a football team within its community, but it certainly never made it to the Premier

239

League. That modern construct has undoubtedly brought prosperity of a sort, which can be reflected on a balance sheet, but in doing so it has changed the game and its character forever. Many will argue that much of that change has been for the better and that such an ingrained element of our society is bound to progress in tandem with that world as it evolves. Times are indeed altered, but trade's unfeeling train has had its effect on the modern game of football and there are some things that have undoubtedly decayed. A little more rural mirth and a few more manners would be welcome.

That connection between club and people may remain strong for the devoted fans of today but it's altered, and that relationship is more distant in so many ways. For Auburn, read Ipswich, Southampton or Nottingham Forest, or any other scattered hamlet that had the opportunity to rise and heighten the community around it in days gone by. They remain with us and in fleeting moments of success they may come again, but the definition of success hereafter has been adjusted and in terms of relevance to football's unwelcoming top table such clubs and places have, like Goldsmith's village, fallen into disuse. Theirs is a loss that can't be replaced but it's one that those who have taken over in these different times, and now have a responsibility for the souls of such clubs, would do well to acknowledge and pay due respect to what has gone before. Sometimes, sadly, that seems a forlorn hope.

'His legacy went beyond the business of winning trophies.' So says Duncan Hamilton of Brian Clough and he recalls Clough's final match and farewell in 1993 as being 'a raw demonstration of the emotional attachment which existed – and will always exist – between him and his public'. It would be a crime to forget that connection or let it slip away. We should do all three men the service of remembering and valuing what they left behind.

That European ban of 1985 was a pivotal moment in the English game's evolution alongside the Bradford fire that had immediately preceded it and the Hillsborough tragedy four years later. It was never to be the same again, demanding as it did a reset that would ultimately lead to all-seater stadiums, the Premier League and the broadcasting agreements that were to change the relationship between the game, the fans and their players forever. The more intimate nature of that relationship at the time of McMenemy, Clough and Robson was nowhere better exemplified than at their three provincial football clubs. It didn't come about by chance, and it wasn't sustained without deliberate cultivation.

It's right to acknowledge that today football clubs do their best to connect through the work of their 'Football in the Community' schemes. But that's just what they are: schemes – products of the marketing department rather than the managers and players themselves. Of course, the players do their bit when asked – many very genuinely and with real impact – but that's somehow different. In 1975–85 there were no such manufactured community projects – the connection between the public and their club was more natural, organic and close. Football is a very different beast now. The residual regret is that it can't ever be the same again – either the achievement of such sustained results on the pitch in the face of the big getting bigger, or the special nature of that bond between players and fans.

Of course, plenty of supporters still follow their hometown club with a passion, but as the chances of the vast majority of those hometown clubs winning the big prizes continue to recede every year, young fans increasingly base their allegiance on the club with the best chance, or their favourite player, or the level of media noise around that club, and a connection to a hometown club is no longer necessarily the determining factor. Tim Smith has his own vision of the future of football-following, which doesn't include that special bond with the place you're from: 'These days young kids don't value their hometown via football. They'll end up supporting City.' It would be pointless to suggest they should feel guilty as a result. It's simply a different world and many digest their football in a different way. So be it.

The relationship has changed. We're unlikely to see Bruno Fernandes putting down his roots in Salford come retirement, or N'Golo Kanté and Riyad Mahrez making Leicester their lifelong homes. Nor do I see much chance of the Manchester City players sitting on the train with their fans on the way back from a cup quarter-final sharing a few cans in the manner of the Saints team of 1976. This isn't their fault – it's just the way it is, and the game and times have moved on, some parts for the better but with much of the value lost along the way. Whatever happens in the future, nobody else will ever be able to deliver Southampton's first-ever FA Cup, Ipswich's first FA Cup and European trophy, or Forest's first domestic and European titles. It only ever happens once. The men who made it happen are simply too good to be forgotten and have a lasting legacy.

Mick Channon is in no doubt:

> It's what's left behind now … you hand it down. All my kids are Southampton supporters. It's passed on and that's where the support comes from. They aren't going today because of the atmosphere at St Mary's. Our time made Southampton and the club what it is today. Owners will come and go but the fans will always be there.

And reflecting on the cup final and the years that followed, Channon makes the point:

> We must never forget that a football club belongs to the people, not to any specific person or persons. You support a football club from your heart. The heart of Southampton is the fans – directors, players and

managers are just caretakers. Southampton FC will
survive because it has a heart.

Whether that heart is in the same health today is another
matter. The importance of the connection between manager,
players, fans and community in those years is evident in the
sense of bitterness detectable in one former Saints player's
assessment of what has changed for him at the club today
and his regret at the perception of arrogance and the apparent
ambivalence towards the fans who still have a huge pride in
those teams of the past. For someone who grew up watching
him play more than 400 times for Southampton it's sad to
hear Steve Williams, admittedly in his characteristically
unconcerned manner, suggest today that one of the reasons he
doesn't get together with his old Saints colleagues as often as
he might, and socialises instead at his boyhood club Arsenal,
is not to make a point but simply because 'Arsenal ask me.
Southampton don't. They seem friendlier somehow.'

Although the new ownership at Ipswich suggests improved
future prospects, already borne out by an overdue promotion
from League One, there's a sense that the new regime doesn't
really want to be reminded of the past. This has echoes of
periods at Southampton when, in the Lowe and Cortese years
in particular, many former players as well as McMenemy were
treated with something approaching disdain. The removal of
all vestiges of the McMenemy years at Southampton at that
time predicated on a 'we don't live in the past here' mentality
may have been an attempt to radiate strength and ambition,
but it was at best ham-fisted and surely ill-advised at a club
that had built a genuine mutual affection with the supporters
who attended matches and the residents of the city itself.
To see such a past as a threat rather than something to be
celebrated is a misjudgement that reflects well on nobody. It's
not an approach that will wash with the fans, who will always
cherish and value the memories of what their managers made

real and will therefore offer them their lifelong devotion. Tim
Smith again:

> We played Bristol Rovers a few weeks ago and I had
> a new guy working for me. I took him to a game at
> Portman Road and the first thing I did was show him
> the Sir Bobby Robson statue and the one of Kevin
> Beattie because I wanted to show him, and for him
> to understand, what the history of this club was. The
> success of the club in that time – nobody thought that
> could happen to a club like Ipswich. When you look at
> the population and demographic, we would get crowds
> of 30,000-plus and if you consider a population of the
> town of around 100,000 and a wider catchment of, say,
> 200,000, that's a significant proportion. The town and
> the club were inextricably linked back then.

The shame is that this airbrushing out of the greatest periods
in the clubs' histories simply isn't necessary and says more
about the perpetrators than the victims. Football isn't a
happy place if it feels recognition of past achievements and a
welcoming of those involved with them is a sign of weakness
or lack of direction. Those who were there will always retain
a special, very personal affection for that time and no amount
of revisionism or eradication will change that. In the end,
the three football communities would never be able to repay
the service they had from these men but to not even try is a
shameful dereliction, the root of a heresy.

Perhaps the reason it happens is because those now in
charge are well aware it's not something that will happen again,
under their watch or anybody else's. One former Southampton
player, who shall remain anonymous, had a recent experience
there that left him feeling 'that's not the club I grew up with',
which is the greatest sorrow at the end of this story. Such
owners might like to reflect on the words of such a dedicated

fan as Tim Smith: 'When a community doesn't have that dream, that ambition, because there will always be a financial ceiling now, that's sad. But for me, we'd rather underachieve in terms of the pyramid and have our own club than have success through investment that simply isn't relevant to our people and community.' In the exalted levels of football where the Champions League is regarded as an economic necessity, the achievements of my own club in those years gone by might even be regarded as failure. It didn't feel that way to me.

Bobby Robson suggested late in his career that clubs who sell their best players to cover costs are unlikely to find themselves playing Real Madrid in a Champions League Final anytime soon. That this course of action is now inevitable for such clubs rankles with Steve Williams, whose frustration may be considered an attempt at urination into a strong gale in today's reality, but who insists, 'In those days you brought players through the youth system to play for, and give back *to*, the club, not to be sold to make money *for* the club.' These three clubs were able to retain their best players for a time, primarily as we have seen through the charisma and abilities of their managers, in a way that smaller clubs who have success today simply cannot do. So, Leicester may defy the odds to win the Premier League once, but they can't sustain a position at the top table because the big boys come calling. Even if they then recruit well, it becomes an ongoing cycle.

Did the three managers keep these players together through their powers of personality or their promise of success? The key was that although the money on offer at that time was still often better elsewhere, it wasn't as life-changing, and these players genuinely believed they could win the big trophies where they were – with many believing this would be a more significant accomplishment. When the managers left, the players lost that feeling and gradually departed as well, and the era was over. It's with an air of sadness that Viv Anderson concedes in the documentary *I Believe in Miracles* that 'in this day and age, whoever gets promoted now, going up and winning it [the title]? No, it'll never happen again.' Duncan Hamilton makes the same point: 'No other Brian Clough could emerge from the swamp of banknotes that is modern football … no team from a backwater is capable of gaining, let alone sustaining, a competitive edge over clubs that are run as vast corporations.' And that's the nub of it – we've moved from communities to corporations, and in the process the balance of power has moved from the manager's office to the players in the dressing room. It's not a scenario in which Clough, Robson or McMenemy could have used the same methods and achieved the same result, nor indeed one in which they would even have wanted to try.

In suggesting that their achievements wouldn't be possible again today, that doesn't mean they didn't leave their own legacies for the modern game and those who manage within it. The list of names who credit them with their own development and approach reads like a *Who's Who* of modern football management. So many took something from them, with Robson being perhaps the best example. Jose Mourinho is clear that 'without his trust I couldn't have jumped so fast to deal with the best players in the world'. Sir Alex Ferguson also acknowledges a debt to a man he held in the highest esteem, noting that he was generous with his time, especially in supporting young managers and that his approach to people was different to the managers of Ferguson's own time. Robson invited him to one of his training sessions and Ferguson admits, 'I took a lot out of what he did that day.' Today, Pep Guardiola is renowned for the team spirit he engenders and the strength of the relationships he builds with his players. How to achieve this, through communication and feedback, he insists is something he learned directly from working under Robson.

These clubs were their people, and the people were the clubs. All three men made these places their homes and their old players often their lifelong friends. In the end each will forever remain connected to the places they revolutionised. In my time working for the sports company adidas, they had a vision statement that 'sport has the power to change lives'. It may sound like a bit of me-too marketing speak but its truth was borne out in these communities all those years ago. Lives were genuinely changed. Martin O'Neill is referring to the city as much as the dressing room when he says, 'There was a change when that man stepped into Nottingham,' and his team-mate Ian Bowyer says of the city, 'It affected everybody – touched everybody. People going into work were a lot happier than they were five years previously.' That alone is not a bad legacy to put your name to. For those who lived it, it was a truly memorable experience.

In *The Ultimate Patriot*, Bob Harris poses a rhetorical question: 'The words "Bobby Robson" and "Ipswich Town" are synonymous, aren't they? He and his wife Elsie were considered part of the fabric of the town.' The fabrics of Ipswich, Southampton and Nottingham will always contain more than a thread of Bobby Robson, Lawrie McMenemy and Brian Clough. And so they should.

Finally, they shouldn't be forgotten because they were just so darned good and they leave an invaluable management handbook for those to come. Robson felt, 'For the area, to bring success at a European level to a little market town like Ipswich, is quite a feat.' Clough is considered by many to be the greatest English manager in history, while Gary Lineker votes for Robson: 'If you consider what he's done, I would say he's the best English manager of all time.' The player who was the common denominator across all McMenemy's creations at Southampton, Nick Holmes, is well qualified to suggest 'those nine or ten years were like a dream and Lawrie was the whole reason it happened. You cannot take that away from him,' while full-back Ivan Golac suggested one of the main reasons he agreed to join the club was that at the time McMenemy and Brian Clough were the two managers in the English game most admired abroad. It's not their fault, of course, merely a confirmation of their abilities should you need another proof that those who tried to follow in their footsteps at all three clubs wouldn't get within any measurable distance of them.

I call to the witness stand Steve Brookes and his testimony in his introduction to *The Fans Behind the Legend*. Nottingham native and Forest fan, he says simply of Clough:

> Before him they had struggled for years, regarded as also-rans who would never threaten the dominance of the more fashionable sides. After him they have endured seasons of underachievement. But during his time in charge, he won nearly everything and reached heights it would have been impossible to imagine attaining under any other manager. For a humble city from the East Midlands to join the elite was an achievement that seems almost impossible to modern eyes.

These concluding thoughts are perhaps a paean for what football was, and maybe should be, but we all know it's now too late for that. This is why to remember that time is important – those days, and the three men who delivered them, were too good to be forgotten and should forever be treated as such.

* * *

A final, personal appreciation. If you combine the completely unexpected success of my football club with what feels like a much simpler world at that time, and the best music era of my life (the best era *always* being anyone's teenage years, admittedly), a certain nostalgia on my part is, I hope, understandable and explains my interest in the impact of what was achieved on the life of many a football follower and player of the time, leaving indelible memories and a debt of gratitude to the men who made it happen, which endures today. Therefore, I can offer no apology for the nostalgia for, and trumpeting of, the football years of 1975 to 1985, three very special football men and their last-ever true breaking of the football mould.

Author's Note

Although being the author of a book involves a certain amount of hard work, the benefit is that you have carte blanche to choose the content – admittedly in the hope that others may ultimately find that content interesting but, nonetheless, the topic and the narrative are yours to dictate – what to include and what to leave out. I accept that some may challenge the approach or see possible omissions – we football fans can be a parochial bunch. It's unlikely there has ever been much purely objective writing on a footballing era of some distance; most of those who love the game enough to undertake such a task will retain loyalties to teams, players and seasons past. I attempted to offset the inevitable subjectivity of my own involvement as a fan in this era by including the views and recollections of others – fans and players alike – to supplement my own. Duncan Hamilton may have given the best description of the task of reporting on and writing about football when he called it 'intelligent guesswork … trying to understand what is happening from the evidence – first-hand or empirical – gathered from various sources'. This is what I've striven to do with this analysis. But with the objective content inevitably comes the subjective if you were around when it was happening. I offer therefore an explanation of the choices I made for *Too Good to Be Forgotten*.

Why these three?

It's true that other managers within their peer group have rightly been feted for their own achievements – another man of the North East, Bob Paisley, won more trophies at Liverpool in the period on which we focus. Ron Saunders won as many major trophies (and as good as added one more) as Bobby Robson and Lawrie McMenemy combined at this time, so why no Aston Villa? They also contributed between 1975 and 1982 to a greater variety of names on trophies and their exclusion and that of their manager from this analysis is not to ignore the two League Cups, one title and, remarkably, one European Cup that they brought home, and I hereby acknowledge these with my apologies to those who spend many of their weekends half a mile off the A38. Villa were and remain, however, a big-city club and had a heritage that included titles, cups (indeed at one point the five FA Cup triumphs were a record) and significant national recognition, and as such don't quite fit the narrative. Paisley was a legendary manager; Saunders undoubtedly a successful one. But it's arguable that, given the status and resources of the clubs they took to unexpected glory (and in Paisley's case the health in which he found Liverpool on taking over from Bill Shankly), the feats of Clough, Robson and McMenemy, particularly in this ten-year period from 1975 to 1985, were even greater and perhaps, for McMenemy at least, less heralded than they should be.

Why these three clubs and the ten-year span used to define the glory days?

It's true that the three managers' careers at Ipswich, Southampton and Nottingham Forest specifically, and the sweet spots of their success, didn't start and end at exactly the same times. Bobby Robson's reign at Ipswich Town began six years before this pseudo-decade of 1975–85, and Brian Clough's tenure at Forest lasted for eight years beyond it. The actual period in which the three were in charge at these clubs concurrently runs only from Clough's arrival in January 1975 to Robson's departure for England in the summer of 1982. These were the years during which they were at the peak of their powers and delivered between them two promotions, one league title, two FA Cups, three European trophies (excluding such frivolities as Super Cups) and two League Cups. But it feels more suitable to focus on these ten years for several reasons. They begin with Clough's arrival at Forest and end at McMenemy's decision that finally the time was right to leave Southampton. Even though Robson was gone by 82, Clough and McMenemy continued to achieve. Clough did so rather more erratically, his domestic success atrophying over the following three years via some strange and what he referred to as 'complacent' transfer moves. He still managed, from the ashes, to create a new, young team that made another, and last, European semi-final in 1984 (which Clough and all Forest fans would swear forevermore should have been a final). That same season McMenemy had constructed another team fit to challenge at the very top, which actually had his team tilting at the double. So McMenemy leaving Southampton for Sunderland in the summer of 1985 seems the right place to draw the curtain down on the glory days.

Why care?

The three managers came from places and upbringings that instilled in them a deep understanding of the worth of the impact their achievements had on their wider communities. It never left them, for all the trophies it's their most lasting legacy, and it's the theme running like a river through their story. I don't believe it can ever happen this way again and it mattered to me that it shouldn't be forgotten.

In the end this is why I felt that this was a tale worth telling. That of Forest, Saints and Ipswich, and of Brian Clough, Lawrie McMenemy and Bobby Robson.

References

Interviews

Players

Southampton:

Peter Rodrigues

Mick Channon

Hughie Fisher

Paul Bennett

Steve Williams

Nottingham Forest

Tony Woodcock

John McGovern

Ipswich

Bryan Hamilton

Allan Hunter

Russell Osman

John Wark

Media

Bob Harris

Fans
Tim Smith
David Dykes
Richard Collier
Michael Channon Jnr

Bibliography

Batt, Peter, *Mick Channon: The Authorised Biography* (Highdown, 2004).

Brookes, Steve, *Brian Clough: The Fans Behind the Legend* (Empire, 2015).

Bull, David, *Match of the Millennium: The Saints' 100 Most Memorable Matches* (Hagiology, 2000).

Clarke, Gabriel, *Bobby Robson – More than a Manager* (documentary, Noah Media Group, 2018)

Clough, Brian, *Clough: The Autobiography* (Partridge Press, 1994).

Crook, Alex, *Match of My Life: Southampton* (Pitch, 2014).

Hamilton, Duncan, *Provided You Don't Kiss Me: 20 Years with Brian Clough* (Harper Perennial, 2008).

Harris, Bob, *Bobby Robson: The Ultimate Patriot* (De Coubertin, 2020).

Harris, Bob, *Sir Bobby Robson: A Life in Football* (Weidenfeld & Nicholson, 2009).

Hunt, Terry, *Ipswich Town FC: The 1970s – The Glory Years Begin* (Archant Regional, 2010).

Ipswich Town: The Boys of '81 (documentary, VSI Enterprises Ltd, 2011).

Keegan, Kevin, *My Life in Football* (Pan Macmillan, 2018).

Manns, Tim, *Tie a Yellow Ribbon: How the Saints Won the Cup* (Hagiology, 2006).

McMenemy, Lawrie, *A Lifetime's Obsession* (Sport Media, 2016).

McMenemy, Lawrie, *The Diary of a Season* (Arthur Barker, 1979).

Moynihan, Leo, *The Three Kings* (Quercus, 2020).

Osgood, Peter, *Ossie: King of Stamford Bridge* (Mainstream, 2002).

Rayvern Allen, David & Arlott, John, *Another Word from Arlott* (London, Guild, 1985).

Robson, Bobby, *Farewell but Not Goodbye: My Autobiography* (Hodder & Stoughton, 2009).

Taylor, Daniel, *I Believe in Miracles* (Headline, 2016).

Van Hulsen, Tom, *Game Changers: The Remarkable Story of Dutch Masters Arnold Mühren and Frans Thijssen* (Portman Road Productions, 2017).